A Post-Christendom Faith I

A Post-Christendom Faith I

THE LONG BATTLE FOR THE HUMAN SOUL

Philip A. Rolnick

BAYLOR UNIVERSITY PRESS

Waco, Texas 76798

Cover and book design by Kasey McBeath

The Library of Congress has cataloged this book under ISBN 978-1-4813-0892-2.
Library of Congress Control Number: 2021936326

This volume, *The Long Battle for the Human Soul*, is volume 1 of a set of three volumes comprising *A Post-Christendom Faith*.

Printed in the United States of America on acid-free paper with a minimum of thirty percent recycled content.

In memoriam

Javier Sanmiguel
(1988–2019)
A beloved husband and father who died heroically while aiding others.

CONTENTS

ACKNOWLEDGMENTS

As I wrote the chapters of *The Long Battle for the Human Soul*, I remained in conversation with friends, some nearby and some far away. As these friends read the chapters, and as we discussed various issues, I benefited greatly from their expertise and insight. For their assistance and for the high pleasure generated by friends pursuing truth together, I am grateful to all of them.

Jeffrey Wattles, formerly professor of philosophy at Kent State University, made invaluable suggestions and criticisms on issues great and small. Reinhard Hütter, professor of theology at the Catholic University of America, shared many insights about Nietzsche and his influence. Richard Crane, professor of history at Benedictine College, and historian Fr. Michael Keating shared a wealth of information and understanding about the history of the West. Ray Mackenzie, professor of English and my colleague at St. Thomas, provided helpful advice about Romantic literature.

I am also indebted to a local group of colleagues and friends that we call, après C. S. Lewis, J. R. R. Tolkien, et al., "The Thinklings." This group often meets to share a meal and discuss a chapter or article that one of us has written. These friends include: Walter Schultz, former professor of philosophy at University of Northwestern in the Twin Cities; Lisanne Winslow, who has doctorates in biology and theology and is professor of biology at Northwestern (and Lisanne's daughters

Arianna and Sophia); Amanda Post and Kayla Sanmiguel, remarkably talented former students; and Dave Deavel, my colleague at St. Thomas, who is professor of theology in Catholic Studies and editor of the journal *Logos*.

I would like to thank Rita Kateri-Hipp and Rachel Rautio for their assistance in producing the index.

Additionally, I am in various ways indebted to John Boyle, Jeanne Buckeye, Mike Naughton, Paul Gavrilyuk, Deborah Savage, John Martens, and Robert Kennedy. Finally, heartfelt thanks to David Aycock, Cade Jarrell, and the entire team at Baylor University Press. They are very good at what they do, and they are a delight to work with.

INTRODUCTION

A House-to-House Battle

> Ever since its foundation—Christianity has never ceased to be assailed; but not always from the same quarter, nor by the same type of adversary, nor with the same weapons.
>
> **Henri de Lubac**[1]

It was a most unusual success. Somehow, a handful of minimally educated Galilean fishermen set in motion the transformation of the Western world, as they and their successors presented the story of the incarnation of the Son of God, his teachings, death, and resurrection. As the transformation took several centuries to spread throughout Europe, Asia Minor, and Northern Africa, and several more to spread to the rest of the world, the story of Jesus became the central story of countless lives—the story that bestowed meaning, value, and purpose.

Christianity in part succeeded because its adherents were not only given a new way to understand God and their world, they were also given an identity, a new way to understand themselves. From Jesus' "Our Father" prayer, Christians understood themselves as sons or daughters of God, an identity reinforced by the Apostle Paul: "For all who are led by the Spirit of God are children of God. . . . When we cry, 'Abba! Father!' it is that very Spirit bearing witness with our spirit that we are children of God" (Rom 8:14, 15b-16). As children of God Christians also saw themselves made "in the image of God" (Gen 1:26-27). In each of these scriptures human identity is defined in terms of relation to God. The truth about humanity—individually, collectively, and historically—is known through relationship to God. Our existence is not accidental; it is chosen by the Creator of the universe.

But if human identity is made in the image of God and realized in relationship to God, what happens when many people cease to believe that the Deity is actually interested in humanity? Or more extremely, what happens if it is believed that there is no Deity, that human origin is an accidental development of an accidental universe? The belief or assumption that humanity is entirely on its own has variously been called "exclusive humanism," "secular humanism," or "atheistic humanism." Whatever their distinctions, each of these focuses on the immanent—what is accessible in such things as nature, culture, education, politics, and economics. By contrast, the focus of Christianity and Judaism is expanded to include God as the transcendent cause of nature and all that subsequently comes into existence. Wholly immanent views tend to assume that nature is its own explanation and seek only scientific explanations about phenomena within nature. Christianity and Judaism explain the very existence of nature and humanity by a Creator God—a transcendent cause outside the universe.[2] For human identity the distinction is stark. In immanental humanisms, humanity must fashion its own identity and place within the natural world; in Christian faith, human identity and purpose, what is most important about humanity, is already given to us by God.

Over the last five hundred years or so there has been a rise in exclusive humanism. As Charles Taylor points out, in the early 1500s it was difficult not to believe in God; now belief is merely one option among many. Given multiple options from which to choose, our situation is not simply a battle between Christian faith and atheistic humanism; it is more like a "free-for-all."[3] The battle for the human soul, including whether or not there is a human soul, has become a house-to-house, and even an in-house struggle. Competing positions are now commonly taken by husbands and wives, parents and children, classmates, and coworkers. Concerning the purpose of human life, we live in an age where little can be taken for granted.

The failure to understand the competing trajectories of our current context and something of how we arrived at this point comes at a cost. Christian faith has been radically questioned; full-blown attacks have been undertaken; and secular alternatives have been proposed. In our context of multiple religious options, it is easy to become perplexed about what matters most. People of traditional Christian faith, people of no faith, and even those who define themselves as "spiritual but not religious" can make better sense of the present by taking stock of the movements that have formed and deformed our self-understanding. Even the anti-theist Auguste Comte (1798–1857) recognized the need to put disputes into historical context: "No idea can be properly understood apart from its history."[4] How to understand faith in Christ, share it, and defend it now require some working knowledge of how we got into our contemporary free-for-all.

Historical criticisms, alternatives, and attacks against Christian teaching have led to a range of developments, including reliance upon reason alone, as in the Enlightenment; exclusive, atheistic humanism, as in Comte and Ludwig Feuerbach; atheistic rejection of both Christianity and humanism, as in Friedrich Nietzsche; revolutionary and even murderous devotion to political arrangements, as in the French and Russian revolutions; and nihilism, the rejection of any meaning, value, or purpose.

Our age is too complex to describe with a single term or phrase. There are millions living lives of faith,* service, and love; millions who are drifting, unhappy, and confused; and millions more who are trying to create their own category, like "spiritual but not religious." Increasingly shrill disputes about education, culture, politics, and economics are inevitable when so many have so many different views about more basic issues.

By theologically examining some of the historical developments of the last five hundred years, including the alternatives to Christian teaching, we can look again—or for the first time—at the Christian teaching that we are sons and daughters of the Creator and made in the divine image. A great deal is at stake in this examination, for as C. S. Lewis put it, "Christianity is a statement, which, if false, is of *no* importance, and, if true, of infinite importance. The one thing it

* Throughout this book "faith" will be used as an umbrella term that includes wide applications among those who are Catholic, Protestant, and Orthodox. Depending on context, it can refer to the body of Christian teachings, the believer's act of accepting those teachings, or the believer's act of trusting God.

cannot be is moderately important."[5] With the hope of confirming, broadening, and deepening Christian faith in those who have it, and with the further hope of inviting others into faith, let us now examine some of the historical criticisms, alternatives, and attacks.

1
CRITICAL TURNS
Reformation, Enlightenment, and Revolution

> Why is it so hard to believe in God in (many milieux of) the modern West, while in 1500 it was virtually impossible not to?
> **Charles Taylor**

> Our age is, in especial degree, the age of criticism, and to criticism everything must submit.
> **Immanuel Kant**

> To laicize the Gospel, to keep the human aspirations of Christianity but do away with Christ—is not all this the whole essence of the Revolution? . . . It was Jean-Jacques [Rousseau] who completed that amazing performance.
> **Jacques Maritain**

> But if it was a time of freedom and hope, it was also a time of illusion.
> **Christopher Dawson on the French Revolution[1]**

There are numerous ways to understand the prodigious changes over the last five hundred years in the West, but from a theological, religious point of view, the Reformation, Enlightenment, and French Revolution stand out as turning points. Each of these historical events has in common a radical critique of authority, whether of the church† or of political, social, or economic affairs. From the early 1500s to the end of the eighteenth century, there was a crescendo of critique: the Reformation's faith-based criticism in turn led to the Enlightenment's reason-based criticism, which in turn led to the radical reformulations and dramatic events of the French Revolution.

† Aside from a few contexts in which a particular denomination is under discussion, "church" will be used not just to refer to the communion to which I belong (the Roman Catholic Church), but instead will be used in a broad, ecumenical sense.

While Catholics and Protestant Reformers still agreed that human identity is determined in relation to God, the Enlightenment and the French Revolution moved toward exclusively humanistic self-understandings, toward understanding humanity and its undertakings apart from God. In a broad, social sense, attempting to understand the world and humanity apart from God was unprecedented. This secularized humanism directed its attention to the immanent, tangible experience of nature and human society. It tended to leave aside or overtly reject the transcendent. Instead of understanding humanity as made in the image of God, a self-understanding that combines transcendence and immanence, secular humanism focused solely on the immanent, pouring its energy into reshaping social and political structures.

Over a little less than a three-hundred-year period, the West successively underwent the earthshaking developments of the Reformation, Enlightenment, and French Revolution. The Reformation was begun as an effort to restore Christian faith; the Enlightenment and the Revolution were, generally speaking, attempts to break away from Christian faith. At the onset of the Reformation, for many centuries the church had been the most perduring, most central, and most important institution of the Western world. Once its structural unity was broken, other kinds of breakage, once unthinkable, would follow—the progressive dismantlings of the Enlightenment and the Revolution.

Reformation

After the fall of the Western Roman Empire (often dated as AD 476), with the progressive weakness of Rome's secular authorities, the bishops of Rome took on much of the ruling authority of the capital city. By the pontificate of Gregory the Great (590–604), responsibility for social, economic, and political questions had fallen upon church leadership; and by the mid-eighth century, the bishops of Rome actually became rulers of entire Italian territories, the Papal States. Amid the catastrophic upheavals of barbarian invasions of the fourth and fifth centuries, and then again of Viking, Magyar, and

Muslim invasions of the ninth and tenth centuries, the church provided stability and a path forward. Repeatedly, as Thomas E. Woods observes, in times of widespread destruction, "The Church, as the educator of Europe, was the one light that survived."[2]

Nevertheless, over the following centuries, as its medieval bureaucracy extended, the church often faltered in its attempt to live up to Jesus' vision. In historian Brad S. Gregory's assessment, "The church as a whole and in practice never closely resembled the kingdom of God proclaimed by Jesus, despite the way in which late medieval theologians self-flatteringly tended to identify the two. In fact, by the fourteenth century, the *more* the church lengthened its bureaucratic reach and influence, the *less* did it look like the kingdom."[3] For the church, the danger was that involvements of secondary import, valuable as they may have been, could divert the body of Christ from its greater and primary purpose.

As early as the twelfth century, with Joachim of Fiore (1135–1202), and continuing all the way up to Martin Luther (1483–1546), devout voices rose up to protest the discrepancy between the church's sacred calling and its actual state. Dante Alighieri (c. 1265–1321) called for the church to yield its secular power. John Wyclif and John Hus contrasted the very imperfect reality of the visible church to the true, invisible church of Christ.[4] In 1512, just before the strife with Luther, Giles of Viterbo, leader of the Augustinian order, opened the Fifth Lateran Council by declaring that the problem was not what was being taught, but rather that so many were not living up to Christ's teachings.[5] From the eleventh to the sixteenth century, earnest Reformers attempted to awaken leaders and laity to their calling; and especially during the fifteenth century, there was a period of growing lay devotion.

By contrast, the popes immediately preceding Luther's times simply failed to recognize the sacred responsibility of their office. They instead indulged in "venality, luxury, and blatant violations of Christian morality at the papal court."[6] Unfortunately, this papal failure was in various ways shared by many cardinals, bishops, and priests. Burdened with these flaws of leadership, the church was vulnerable to the extremely serious challenge that Luther would bring.

Luther was a gifted Augustinian monk trained by the church in biblical languages. In 1517 he posted ninety-five theses about the nature of faith and church practice, a kind of challenge that was in those days not uncommon. But as his theses were disputed, something quite uncommon came to pass: his criticism of church teaching and practice became a revolt against church authority. Luther did not originally intend to break the unity of the Western church and start a church of his own; but when the controversy reached a breaking point, he refused to recant and refused to be silenced. With the support and protection of various German princes, the Protestant Reformation was launched.

Our present task is not to adjudicate Lutheran or Catholic theology or their differing understandings of church practices. Our more modest (and irenic) task is merely to recognize the cataclysmic effects of this unexpected and, at least at first, involuntary shattering of the church's unity.

Unintended Consequences

In the West, once a second Christian church had been established, even within Luther's lifetime other Protestant movements arose that opposed both Catholicism and Luther. All the non-Catholic Reformers agreed on the basic principle of *sola scriptura*, but intractable problems arose in how to interpret scripture. Attempts to solve disputes by appealing to the guidance of the Holy Spirit made disagreements more heated, since neither party was likely to own that it was not inspired by the Holy Spirit. All Protestant groups agreed in refusing the authority of the Roman Catholic Church, but they could not agree about eucharist, baptism, and social/political engagement. Having discarded the authority of Rome, there was no way to adjudicate disagreements. Hostilities among Lutheran, Reformed, Anabaptist, Mennonite, and other smaller sects became intense, as did opposition between Luther and Huldrych Zwingli, one of the most vigorous and powerful of the early Reformers. When Zwingli wrote, "I know for certain that God teaches me, because I have experienced it," Luther replied, "Beware of Zwingli and avoid his books as the hellish poison of Satan . . . , for the man is completely perverted . . . and has completely lost Christ."[7] The times were polemical and dangerous; it was easy to be exiled or to lose one's life for one's beliefs. Nuance, tolerance, and striving to hear the other's point of view were not the order of the day.

One of the most regrettable outcomes was an insoluble hyperpluralism that has never gone away.[8] Disagreements arose about whether doctrinal truth claims even mattered, as some would-be prophets and "spiritualists" thoroughly relativized the place of doctrine.[9] Disparity of religious belief in turn bred fierce social, political, and economic disagreements. The roots of our current relativism were established, as the highly contentious, pluralist environment led to the question that still remains: Who's to say who's right?

Luther's rebellion against church authority all too quickly led to a different kind of conflict, the Peasant Rebellion of 1524–1525. While Luther recognized that the peasants had some just complaints, he had no love for radicals or revolutionaries. He commendably attempted to broker a peaceful resolution to the conflict between tens of thousands of German peasants, the landed aristocracy, and wealthy merchants. When his efforts to achieve peace failed, Luther felt that order had to be restored. He then advised the rulers to take strong measures to suppress the rebellion, and they did.[10] The ensuing battles went badly for the peasants, with over 100,000 killed. In Protestant lands, a new policy of church/state relations was established that implemented Luther's views of the relation between the earthly and the heavenly kingdoms.[11]

In addition to the Peasant Rebellion, a series of other wars broke out among Protestant and Catholic rulers, as well as between Protestants. In the late 1520s and early 1530s in Switzerland, Catholic and Protestant forces clashed. In 1547 the emperor of the Holy Roman Empire, Charles V, defeated the Lutheran Schmalkaldic League but then later suffered reverses, which led to the 1555 Peace of Augsburg, an arrangement that pleased neither side but did manage an uneasy peace. Between 1562 and 1598 French Huguenots and Catholics fought eight civil wars, with religious riots often erupting in between and sporadic hostilities lasting until 1629. In 1566, the Dutch rebelled against the Spanish Catholic Philip II's efforts against heresy, with these hostilities lasting until 1648. In the 1640s in England, Puritan resistance to the Anglican Charles I, in addition to other issues of governance, led to two civil wars. Between 1618 and 1648 much of Europe was afflicted by the Thirty Years War, a complicated affair that involved Catholic versus Protestant as well as various opportunistic reaches for land and power. At the end, besides other European devastation, almost one-third of the German people had perished. The intensity of religious and political disagreement led to warfare, the extensive scope of which was unprecedented in European history.[12]

The formal treaty that ended the Thirty Years War established territorial linkages of church and political authority, both in Catholic lands like Bavaria and in what would be recognized as Protestant lands like Prussia. The formula first used at the 1555 Peace of Augsburg, *cuius regio, eius religio* (whose region, his religion), now provided a more permanent territorial solution, the establishment of confessional states.

In these confessional regimes, whether Catholic, Lutheran, Calvinist, or Anglican, political rulers sanctioned and enforced church doctrine in their respective territories. This concentrated amalgam of church and state provided publicly held expectations of religious belief and morality as well as political obedience. However, the destabilizing problem was that each confessional state had its share of religious dissenters; and under the fusion of church and state, dissenters were often, in one way or another, persecuted.[13] Perhaps a political realm can continue indefinitely with coerced uniformity, but to Jesus' followers, being the partner of coercion will sooner or later prove offensive. The establishment of confessional states may have been the best stopgap solution to chaos and warfare, but the internal contradiction of confessional states would become the target of severe critique. The freedom of the citizens of Christ's kingdom cannot sit comfortably with the coercion of the state. The goal of preserving Christianity as a shared way of life is better relinquished than pursued by force.

The dissonant multiplicity of Christian truth claims led some to question if any of the claims were true. Given the disparity among Christian groups, the exercise of private judgment could claim new validity not previously on offer. With multiple and proliferating church beliefs, it was almost inevitable that individuals would also proliferate their own subjective beliefs, including the belief that God did not exist, or that if there is a God, we cannot know anything true about this Deity.

Criticizing the church from within the church, the Reformation was the first epochal event of criticism. After this critical turn, religious divisions were permanently established, a new map was required, and the hope of quickly reuniting the church was gone. Luther's dispute with church authority began as a substantive disagreement about the nature of faith, an intramural religious argument. But by its end, the dispute splintered the church's unity, and questions about faith, political rule, and their interrelationship spread. The ugliness of protracted warfare led to the fitful arrangement of territorial confessional states, whose internal inconsistencies would soon enough lead to additional religious and societal breakages, as increasingly harsh criticism of the authority of the church—and of what the church taught—opened the door to developments that virtually all the Reformation combatants would have deplored, an unstoppable slippage toward societal secularization.[14] Foundational assumptions had been broken; and in the brokenness, the Enlightenment would launch a second, epochal period of critique.

Enlightenment: Innovations and Disruptions

Reason, Doubt, and Criticism

The Enlightenment period, approximately 1650 to 1800, witnessed new and sometimes shocking proposals about God, scripture, transcendence, the natural world, society, government, and human identity. Enlightenment thinkers also proposed new methods of inquiry and new criteria of what counts as truth. Their innovations disrupted basic assumptions, launching heated debates that continue into our own time. Stretching from Russia to Great Britain and its colonies, the Enlightenment was very much an international phenomenon; but at the same time, it was very differently enacted in different nations.[15] Within each nation and internationally, the Enlightenment altered the course of human history.

In the thirteenth century, Aquinas famously referred to nontheological sciences, including philosophy, as "handmaidens" of theology (*ancillae theologiae*).[16] In the work of René Descartes (1596–1650), and especially Baruch Spinoza (1632–1677), the philosophical handmaid would challenge the mistress for supremacy. Philosophy was increasingly seen as most important, and, intertwined with math and science, as the only matter of importance. The displacement of theology by philosophy was the engine of the Enlightenment movement, which began in the rarified Latin texts of the cognoscenti and quickly spread to wider swaths of the European population.

As Enlightenment ideas permeated Western society, the secularization of the West was accelerated, a secularization that has by now affected every continent and people. The secularizing movement diverted thought and energy toward wholly humanistic concerns, as revolution in thought preceded political and social revolution.

The disruptions and innovations most pertinent to our theological inquiry include the heated debate over Descartes' mechanistic view of nature and new method of starting in doubt; the tumult over Spinoza's rejection of both scriptural reliability and basic Judeo-Christian tenets; increasingly virulent criticism of ecclesial and governmental authority; the advocacy of tolerance for religious minorities; and a secular humanistic devotion to progress.

Descartes: Stirrings of Philosophical Independence

After the initial chaos and strife of the Protestant Reformation, a new stability arose, with four major Western churches—Catholic, Lutheran, Reformed, and Anglican—holding sway in their respective areas. There was some theological sparring among the various churches, but whatever their differences, there was still a general consensus of belief in Christ, which in turn shaped beliefs about nature and humankind. There was also, at least within each confessional regime, consensus about the political and economic spheres. The consensus about belief in God was not disrupted by a frontal assault (frontal assaults would come later), but rather by a dispute about philosophy, especially the dispute between Descartes' philosophy and the venerable Aristotelianism that had become part of both Reformed and Catholic thought.

The Netherlands, where the Frenchman Descartes lived and wrote for twenty years, was renowned for its universities; but these universities developed a contentious split between more conservative thinkers, who had incorporated Aristotelian views into their theology, and more progressive thinkers, who favored Cartesianism.[17] A central point of contention was Descartes' mechanistic view of nature. This view threatened to overturn centuries of previous understanding; and since all agreed that nature had been created by God, the academic, philosophical dispute spilled over into theology. Moreover, Cartesianism challenged the regnant epistemology with one that seemed more conducive to the advancing science of the day.[18] Cartesians rejected the Aristotelian/Thomistic view that all knowledge must come through the senses, as Galileo, Descartes, and many who followed discovered the intelligibility of insensible things like magnetism and gravity. From the epicenter in the Netherlands, Descartes' thought ignited conflict in universities all over Europe. While Descartes held that the existence of God was so certain that "the human intellect cannot know anything that is more evident or more certain,"[19] many who followed did not share this certainty.

Starting Points: Doubt versus Tradition and Faith

Descartes' concern with method was presciently modern. His *Discourse on Method* established ground rules for inquiry that have become assumptions of modern life, even though most are unaware of the Cartesian origin.

Descartes proposed a highly innovative and controversial starting point—to begin by doubting everything that is not provably certain:

> The first [step] was never to accept anything as true that I did not plainly know to be such; that is to say, carefully to avoid hasty

> judgment and prejudice; and to include nothing more in my judgments than what presented itself to my mind so clearly and so distinctly as that I had no occasion to call it into doubt.[20]

Descartes sought basic intuitions that could not be denied without contradiction. His first foundational step requires complete certainty and eliminating anything less than certain. It discounts one's own prejudgments or prejudices; and, strictly observed, it discounts or ignores the prior judgments and wisdom of all others, including those of Jesus, the apostles, and all who followed them in the church tradition.

As a tradition, the church is a historical community motivated to transmit what it has received and has itself accomplished—its articulated beliefs and teachings—across generations. A tradition at its best does not inhibit inquiry; to the contrary, tradition provides inquiry its starting point. Yet in *The Discourse on Method*, Descartes' quest for reliable knowledge (*scientia*) rules out tradition as a starting point.[21] From Descartes to the French Revolution, there is great confidence in the ability to understand all manner of things better than had those in the past.[22]

Although Descartes' method begins in doubt, he was not a skeptic: he began in doubt so that he might end in certainty. Following Descartes, the Enlightenment generally sought knowledge, and often achieved it, through the evolving scientific method in quest of certainty.

There is no problem in seeking certainty where certainty is possible; however, centuries before Descartes, both Aristotle and Aquinas had the wisdom to recognize that, for good reason, different areas of inquiry allow different levels of certainty. As Aquinas wrote, "The slenderest knowledge that may be obtained of the highest things is more desirable than the most certain knowledge obtained of lesser things."[23] As the human mind seeks to know the noblest things, as it seeks to know God, the mind does not achieve mathematical certainty, but it is ennobled by the quest—and by whatever may be discovered or revealed to it.

Quite different from Descartes, it is a Christian commonplace that our inquiries, especially those about God, should begin in faith. Thus the eleventh-century philosopher and theologian Anselm of Canterbury wrote, "For I do not seek to understand that I may believe, but I believe in order to understand. For this also I believe,—that unless I believed, I should not understand." Like Descartes, Anselm recognized that the chosen starting point is crucial. Unlike Descartes, Anselm does not begin in doubt but in faith, coining the phrase that has ever since been one of the great mottoes of Christian theology: "faith seeking understanding."[24]

Not beginning in faith (trust) would actually render humanity incapable of learning. Every child who has ever come into this world, including Descartes, first had to trust parents, relatives, and teachers to impart the rudiments of language. A child that was never spoken to or that somehow doubted its parents' association of words and objects would never learn to speak. A starting point of doubt may work very well for certain kinds of adult endeavors; however, it is empirically demonstrable that for the most basic learning, faith, not doubt, is required. Descartes could not have written his method recommending doubt had he not first trusted the Jesuits to teach him Latin and logic.

Between 1650 and 1720, the international spread of Cartesianism unsettled the universities and then each of the four major churches that were so intertwined with these universities.[25] At the University of Leiden, things got heated between the Cartesians and their Calvinist critics, who claimed that the Cartesian God was no more than a prime mover, a force that sets nature in motion and then has no more to do with it. The state authorities were called into the dispute and enforced a compromise that few applauded but that did establish a temporary working arrangement. In 1676 a renewed controversy took place at the University of Leiden, with the more conservative Calvinists listing twenty objectionable propositions of the Cartesians. Among these was Descartes' method of beginning by doubting everything, even God; the notion that scripture merely speaks to accommodate prejudices of common people; and that philosophy is the valid interpreter of scripture, this last proposition being denied by those accused of holding it. Here again the government had to intrude, with William III upholding the prohibitions on teaching these propositions. But after the initial silencing, a powerful counter-response actually became a bestseller.[26]

Similarly, in Germany Cartesianism was alternately permitted and banned. In France, Louis XIV attempted a compromise: Cartesianism was prohibited in colleges and universities, but Descartes' books could be published.[27] Whatever the best way to understand Descartes may be, his teachings roiled European centers of learning. Not immediately, but within a short time, the suppressed Cartesian faction became the victors.

Spinoza: A Point of No Return

While some saw Descartes as a foe of Christian faith and others saw him as a friend, there was no doubt that Spinoza challenged Christian thought in extraordinary ways. Historian Jonathan Israel writes of Spinoza, "No one else during the century 1650–1750 remotely rivalled Spinoza's notoriety as the chief challenger of the fundamentals of revealed religion, received ideas, tradition, morality, and what was everywhere regarded, in absolutist and non-absolutist states alike, as divinely constituted political authority."[28] Spinoza's disagreements with Judaism (he was excommunicated from the Dutch Synagogue) and his sweeping rejection of Christian beliefs opened the floodgates for increasingly barbed attacks.

In the *Tractatus Theologico-Politicus*, Spinoza identifies God *as* nature, a position that some labeled as atheist, but is more commonly seen as pantheist. Instead of a Creator who transcends nature and sets it in motion in creating it, Spinoza held that motion is eternally inherent in matter. Spinoza's doctrines completely remove divine transcendence and utterly reject the idea of God as Person and Creator. Prayer is pointless, because there is no one who could hear or care about a prayer. There is no will of God except the cause and effect to be discovered in nature. There is nothing divine in scripture, which is merely a compilation of primitive beliefs from primitive people. As Spinoza put it, "The method of interpreting Scripture is not different from the method of interpreting Nature, and is in fact in complete accord with it."[29] Spinoza's view eliminates divine incarnation and resurrection.

There are no miracles, angels, demons, or divine activity on behalf of humanity. Each human person is merely a part in an infinite chain of determined, inflexible causes and effects. The desire to worship a god is entirely psychological, rooted in the determined causes of nature. Hence, religion is merely a deep-seated superstition; mathematics and science constitute the only route to such truth as we can know.[30]

By reducing everything to the causes and effects of nature, Spinoza cut out everything that matters in Christianity. If there is no God who takes an interest in human affairs, then Christianity is a massive and prolonged falsehood that has kept much of the human race locked within its false worldview. Secretly or openly, many came to agree with Spinoza.

Not surprisingly, his philosophical denial of revealed religion led to a public furor. The Leiden Reformed Consistory characterized Spinoza's *Opera Posthuma* as "a book, which perhaps since the beginning of the world until the present day . . . surpasses all others in godlessness and endeavours to do away with all religion and set impiety on the throne."[31] But just as the Reformed Church was unable to contain and suppress Descartes' teachings, so too were they ultimately unable to suppress Spinoza's. Although Spinozists usually denied that they were atheists, whether they were or were not, atheism had become a realistic option.

Although publicly professing atheism in the confessional regimes of the late sixteenth and early seventeenth centuries could still be dangerous, anonymous writers using clandestine publishers put forth shockingly heretical works. Lesser-known figures would often take ideas from philosophers like Descartes, Spinoza, and Thomas Hobbes and go well beyond them into outright disbelief and even mockery of Christian faith. One such notorious work, whose actual author and publisher remained hidden for centuries, was the *Treatise of the Three Imposters* (1719).[32] This work could not have been clearer about its atheism, naturalism, and scorn for religious belief. Impugning Moses, Jesus, and Mohammed as frauds, this work had a revealing alternate title: *The Spirit of Spinoza*. It proclaimed that "those who love the truth" should now repudiate the centuries-old falsehood of a transcendent God;[33]

Jesus was given a scathing assessment; and Jesus' moral teachings were held to include "nothing as useful and sublime as in the writings of the ancient Philosophers."[34] After Jesus' death his apostles were alleged to have fabricated his resurrection and his divine sonship. In the judgment of the treatise, "Christianity like all other Religions is no more than a crudely woven imposture."[35] The early Enlightenment was careening into unexpected and sometimes brazen developments.

Descartes and Spinoza provoked thoroughgoing rethinking, not least of which was philosophy being cut loose from theological service and guidance. From the Spinozists, a new feeling was in the air: Christian faith was old, superstitious, and false; the new philosophy was exciting, daring, and true. After his death Spinoza became something of a cult figure, being referred to as the "virtuous atheist"[36]—the model for many ever since, who so often argue that they can be morally good without belief in God.

Criticism Comes of Age

In the decades following Spinoza, using reason to criticize tradition and authority became an established practice that has continued to our time. Quite different from faith seeking understanding, most Enlightenment thinkers relied on reason alone: they attempted to begin, proceed, and end in reason. Where Luther advocated faith alone (*sola fide*), and then critiqued the authority of the Catholic Church with the authority of the Bible alone (*sola scriptura*), Enlightenment thinkers went further: leaving faith aside, they questioned the historical validity of biblical claims and instead advocated reason alone. From Luther to Descartes to Spinoza to Kant, criticism of external authority deepened and broadened, accelerating down paths that would have repulsed Luther and the other Reformers. Increasingly, authority was placed in one's own self. Advocating the authority of the individual's reason as the way to enlightenment, Kant introduced his famous distinction between heteronomy and autonomy.[37] In heteronomy, someone or something other than the self gives the law; someone other than the self is the authority. The heteronomy could come from a church leader or creed, the Bible, a monarch, a parent, or even a doctor. By contrast, in autonomy the self uses reason to legislate its own law; guided by reason, the self is its own authority.

In advocating autonomy, Kant was well aware that people would stumble and err, but he believed that, eventually, practicing freedom in pursuit of truth would lead to enlightenment. He thus refused to call his own age "enlightened," but he did call it an "age of enlightenment."[38] Enlightenment required freedom to criticize, because criticism of error would open the door to progress—the central motivation of the Enlightenment.

Kant's attempts to critique and thereby improve religion were generally moderate in tone but radical in substance. For him the essence of religion was morality, not grace; real religion begins with what we do, not with what God has done for us:

> Where shall we start, *i.e.*, with a faith in what God has done on our behalf, or with what we are to do to become worthy of God's assistance (whatever this may be)? In answering this question we cannot hesitate in deciding for the second alternative.[39]

Consistently emphasizing human effort and minimizing or eliminating God's action on our behalf, Kant considered the eucharist "a religious illusion which can do naught but work counter to the spirit of religion."[40] Notwithstanding this blunt denial, Kant thought that eucharistic communion was valuable because it pointed participants (Kant himself did not participate) toward moral community and brotherly love.

In *Religion within the Limits of Reason Alone*, a pointed and revealing title, Kant argued, as had Spinoza, against the efficacy of prayer: "*Praying*, thought of as an *inner formal* service of God and hence as a means of grace, is a superstitious illusion . . ."[41] Likewise, Kant contended that using creeds across generations was not just erroneous but

> altogether impossible. Such a contract, made to shut off all further enlightenment from the human race, is absolutely null and void. . . . An age cannot bind itself and ordain to put the succeeding one into such a condition that it cannot extend its . . . knowledge, purify itself of errors, and progress in general enlightenment.[42]

Kant was so dedicated to the possibility of human progress that he called the binding nature of creeds "a crime against human nature."[43]

Although Kant remained respectful of Jesus and the Gospels, his denials of eucharist, prayer, and church creeds were emblematic of the era's ersatz religion of human progress. Kant fully shared the Enlightenment *belief* that reason and criticism, not the church's traditional beliefs and authority, constitute the path to progress. In the wake of the Enlightenment, the belief in reason and the practice of criticism have at best had mixed results and, at worst, been disastrous.

Criticism of the Bible

During the Enlightenment and the years following, a new way of studying the Bible arose—what is now called the historical-critical method. For understanding how our own era came into its moral and religious free-for-all, few developments are as important as the historical-critical approach to the Bible.

It was not necessarily impious to investigate who wrote which parts, when, and under what circumstances, or even to ask whether biblically reported events could be historically verified. However, seminal figures in this movement were motivated by the suspicion that vital biblical claims were fabrications. Coinciding with the rise of modern science, and not unlike Descartes' method, historical-critical scholarship attempted to approach scripture scientifically. Rather than faith seeking understanding, the typical Enlightenment presupposition was naturalistic, believing that only natural events occur in history. From this skeptical starting point, supernatural events like miracles, including Jesus' incarnation and resurrection, were a priori ruled out.

Serious biblical criticism began as early as 1670 with Spinoza; and as the Enlightenment proceeded, the plausibility of the biblical accounts was more and more openly called into question. Catholics and the Eastern Orthodox were certainly affected, but the effects were devastating among Protestants, who had relied so exclusively on biblical authority. For all concerned, a loss of biblical credibility was making Christian faith less plausible. Thus David Hume (1711–1776) famously asked whether a biblically reported miracle was more likely to have occurred, or whether the alleged miracle was more likely to be inaccurate or unreliable testimony from unscientific, naïve people.[44] Miracles increasingly came to be seen as an irrational remnant of a nonscientific, unenlightened age. In this vein, Thomas Jefferson wrote a combined version of the four Gospels that eliminated all miracles and almost all references to the supernatural; but like many other Enlightenment thinkers, Jefferson portrayed Jesus as a great moral teacher.[45] Jefferson, like Kant, remained respectful of Jesus, but more acerbic critics, like the anonymous authors of the *Treatise of the Three Imposters*, contended that one could have either intellectual integrity or Christianity—but not both.

One of these critics was the broadly respected German scholar Hermann Samuel Reimarus (1694–1768). Reimarus considered the purported revelations to the Hebrews to have been fraud, fabrication, and deceit; thought Jesus to have suffered from messianic delusions; and argued that the gospel writers were as deceitful as the earlier Hebrews. Insisting on the Enlightenment commonplace that real religion is based on reason, not dubious claims of revelation, Reimarus' no-holds-barred critique, posthumously published in 1774, stirred great controversy and even caused many to turn away from becoming ministers.[46] Reimarus approached the New Testament like a legal examiner who suspected that something was wrong. Poking and prodding at the four Gospel accounts of the resurrection, he sought to expose contradictions in their details, concentrating on ten that he considered the most egregious.[47] Like critics from the early centuries of Christianity, Reimarus concluded that the apostles had stolen the body at night, but were unable to keep details of the story straight. He asserted that these apostles have received "the poor reputation of their trickery"[48] and that their divergent testimonies would never stand up in a court of law.[49]

If a civilization's religion, morality, and culture have been developed from the believed-in teachings and writings of Jesus' first followers, what happens to that civilization when those known as *Saint* Matthew, *Saint* Mark, or *Saint* Paul are suspected to be fraudulent fabricators?

What Reimarus and others had begun in biblical criticism was brought to heightened public attention in 1835–1836, with the publication in German of David Friedrich Strauss' *The Life of Jesus, Critically Examined*. Adopting the by then well-established method of doubt and reason alone (and deeply influenced by the philosophy of Hegel), Strauss openly questioned whether *any* of the Bible's allegedly supernatural events had taken place. Strauss and many following him held that Jesus was an inspiring teacher, but he was not God incarnate. For them, the resurrection was not a historical event. In Strauss' view, the Jesus of history, the one who actually lived, and the Christ of faith, the one the church believes is the Son of God, are incompatible.

Even today, people are often shocked to learn that many Bible scholars (and many ministers) do not believe that Jesus was divine. Their dismay is understandable, because it is central to Christian belief that the transcendent God penetrated immanent, earthly history in the incarnation, life, death, and resurrection of Jesus. Christianity has always fully affirmed that Jesus was human; in fact, the first heresy (c. AD 140) was the Gnostic denial of Jesus' humanity. But Christianity has equally held that Jesus is divine, that Jesus is both God *and* man. Just as Jesus uniquely linked God and humanity, heaven and earth, the power, persuasiveness, and beauty of Christianity are not simply focused on a transcendent God; but rather, Christianity holds that this transcendent God cares about and has been immanently involved in human affairs—in ancient Israel, in Jesus, and with us. But in Strauss' and others' radical reconfiguration, biblically reported supernatural events were deflated to myth. While the myth may be valuable, it is myth—not history. Many present-day scholars continue to work along a Straussian trajectory. Thoroughly discounting the biblical witness to God's involvement with Israel and advent in Jesus, contemporary biblical scholars also tend to approach the Bible forensically, attempting a quasi-scientific examination to find out what really happened.[50]

While Joseph Ratzinger (Benedict XVI) has recognized the value of historical-critical study of the Bible, he has also urged Bible scholars to avoid "the appearance of a quasi-clinical-scientific certainty" in their conclusions.[51] Biblical exegesis, even the best biblical exegesis, cannot deliver the same kind of certainty as might be achieved in the natural sciences. Instead of this assumed air of scientific certainty, Ratzinger would like Bible scholars to incorporate humility, self-reflection, and self-criticism. The texts that scholars are attempting to understand depict contacts between the natural and supernatural world. To presuppose that there has been no contact, to assume that these texts can only be rightly studied by disbelieving their most important claims, is to decide the most important conclusion of the inquiry before it begins.

Witnesses to shocking events commonly vary in what they remember, and sometimes even present contradictory details. In the shock of seeing a violent crime, witnesses are going to have different reactions, everything from paralyzing fear to coolheaded appraisal of the situation. The shock of witnessing earth's greatest and most unusual event—the resurrection of Jesus—could only have exacerbated normal, subjective human reactions. Yet the biblical witnesses do agree on the major claims: the tomb is empty; Jesus is resurrected. One can take Reimarus' view and accuse all the witnesses of lying; however, if the witnesses were lying, it is striking that they were willing to die—and many did die—for the sake of the alleged lie. Taking on first-century questions about the resurrection, the Apostle Paul succinctly laid out what is at stake: "If for this life only we have hoped in Christ, we are of all people most to be pitied" (1 Cor 15:19). Much of our contemporary unbelief has arisen from the published suspicions that Jesus was not divinely incarnate and was not resurrected, a lack of belief that has now spread to those who have never read the critiques—or the Gospels.

The Critique of Confessional Regimes and Toleration of Religious Minorities

The Enlightenment not only brought severe criticism of church and scripture, it also brought new conceptions of political governance, especially in relation to religious belief and morality. As we have seen, the religious disruption of the Reformation quickly led to violent political disruption; and as the Protestant movement spread and splintered, unmanageable problems and violent eruptions persisted.

The solution of identifying a particular region of land with the church of its ruler (*cuius regio, eius religio*) was sorely tested in France by the presence of a large minority of Calvinist Huguenots. In 1598, Henry IV issued the Edict of Nantes, which granted the minority Protestants civil rights and specified rights of worship. But in 1685, Louis XIV issued the Revocation of the Edict of Nantes, forcing the expulsion of tens of thousands of Huguenots. Although the Revocation was popular in France, elsewhere it greatly offended the rising Enlightenment sensibilities. New conditions had arisen, but the requisite wisdom for dealing with those new conditions was not always manifest.

Like the Huguenots in France, so-called Nonconformist or Dissenter churches were being suppressed in England, as the government attempted to enforce unity with the state-sponsored Anglican Church. In 1685, the same year as the Revocation of the Edict of Nantes, John Locke's *A Letter Concerning Toleration* proposed a solution diametrically opposed to the Revocation: the separation of church and state, and governmental toleration of religious minorities. Locke wrote the letter while he was hiding under an assumed name in Amsterdam. He may have been more than an innocent theorist being unduly oppressed. Locke had fled England in 1683 after being suspected of involvement in a failed attempt to assassinate the king. While he escaped to Holland, one of his accused counterparts, Algernon Sydney, was arrested and then hanged, in spite of rather flimsy evidence against him. Locke had good reason to fear for his life, both for his alleged participation in political rebellion and for his non-trinitarian, deistic religious beliefs, which the Anglican Church considered heretical. The wisdom of the separation of church and state and religious toleration may now seem almost self-evident, but to the confessional states of seventeenth-century Europe these notions were viewed as dangerously radical. Great shifts in human thought and practice do not take place without transitional struggles.

During a transitional time of contention, conflict, outright rebellion, and forceful reprisals, Locke argued that toleration is the mark of the true church, while coercion and state-enforced doctrine reduce the church to the level of empire and ephemeral power.[52] He contended, "The Toleration of those that differ from others in Matters of Religion, is so agreeable to the Gospel of Jesus Christ, and to the genuine Reason of Mankind, that it seems monstrous for Men to be so blind, as not to perceive the Necessity and Advantage of it."[53] Power not only corrupts, it also can blind; and when closely linked to state power, Catholic, Protestant, and Anglican churches had at different times succumbed to such blindness. Once religious pluralism had become an inexpungible reality, it was an Enlightenment achievement—for the health of both church and state—to disentangle their connections and to promote religious tolerance.

The church had long since lost its unity, and a new principle for the new pluralist condition was needed. Locke sensibly proposed that "peace, equity, and friendship" should be practiced among different churches just as they are to be practiced among different persons.[54] He thought it absurd that those whom the gospel had taught to avoid revenge and taught to practice forgiveness when wronged should execute physical or financial punishment on those who disagreed with their religious views. Locke suggested that punishment for deviant religious thinking be left up to God—not enforced by an alliance of church and state: "If each of them would contain itself within its own Bounds, the one attending to the worldly Welfare of the Commonwealth, the other to the Salvation of Souls, it is impossible that any Discord should ever have happened between them."[55] In Western civilization, Locke's views on tolerance and the separation of church and state, once considered dangerous, have become foundational; and under the pluralistic circumstances that have come about, his tolerance-based solution is certainly preferable to religious persecution by the confessional state.[56] However, the terminus of his views, which the West is now broadly experiencing, is that religion and morality have become privatized, formally separated from politics. The movement from the confessional, territorial regime to the secular state is now a fait accompli. But as a result, debate in the public sphere is unguided by commonly accepted transcendent principles, and thereby the public sphere is continuously subject to dangerous riptides of whatever is current. The commendable tolerance of pluralism has more and more given way to the pernicious effects of relativism and subjectivism, at least for those individuals and institutions that have embraced them.

For Christianity the situation is no more perilous than it was in the Roman Empire before Constantine's conversion. The danger and destruction of relativism, secularism, naturalism, and atheism have beset millions and corrupted a wide range of institutions; but Christianity continues apace, not as a public presupposition, but in people and parishes of living faith.

In matters of the soul and the state, coerced uniformity is both morally flawed and misdirected, because the gospel of Christ comes alive by attraction, not by coercion. Moreover, public coercion is inevitably brittle, because any crack can quickly become a calamitous breakage. Tolerating dissent leads to a more durable strength, because the overall unity is more pliant, less likely to shatter at the first disruption. And in human affairs of church and state there are always going to be disruptions. Tolerating criticism is difficult, but it is a civilizing and virtuous practice. In church, state, and every human institution, criticism tends to irritate; but rightly done, it can bring strengthening improvements, alertness, and renewal.

* * *

While the Enlightenment has taken the title "The Age of Reason," it is hardly true that previous ages did not pursue reason. From Heraclitus (535–475 BC) to Aristotle (384–322 BC), the Greeks excelled in developing reason; from Augustine (AD 354–430) to Aquinas (AD 1225–1274) and Duns Scotus (AD 1266–1308), reason flourished in its explication of Creator, cosmos, humanity, and Christ. From the medieval period to the Enlightenment and to the present day, many great scientists have not only been Christians, many were actually monks, priests, bishops, cardinals, or Protestant ministers.[57] The key difference between the Enlightenment and the preceding Christian era is that in Christian thought, reason was housed within a greater context. But in the Enlightenment, reason became the only context and criterion of import.

According to Kant, everything of import, especially religion and government, must prove that it can meet the standards of reason and criticism: "Reason accords [respect] only to that which has been able to sustain the test of free and open examination." For him, criticism was at the heart of the Enlightenment project: "Our age is, in especial degree, the age of criticism, and to criticism everything must submit."[58] That "everything must submit" to critical questioning, to "the test of free and open examination," introduced a new standard that has remained part and parcel of the modern era; questioning every authority and norm has become a common feature of our time. Kant's age was an age of criticism; ours is an age of hyper-criticism. In Kant's, the brightest and most well-educated attempted criticism; in ours, even the illiterate attempt to do so.

In some ways the Enlightenment achieved a commendable form of humanism, as the emphasis on reason led to improvements, at least for a time, in the quality of life in everything from science and technology to music, government, and education. We now take freedoms for granted that Enlightenment thinkers fought for. To us it seems strange that many of Kant's publications had to be submitted to a government censor in Berlin.

In science, a new international community of thought was coalescing around cumulative discoveries focused on this world and how it works. These burgeoning scientific discoveries fed the growing confidence in human ability and, intentionally or unintentionally, contributed to the evolving secular humanism.

Scientists and those who philosophized about science were not necessarily atheists; most were not. But the new ethos of rationalism, bolstered by scientific successes, contributed to the growing tendency of exclusively humanistic thinking. For some minds, the rational wonders being revealed in gravitation, magnetism, chemistry, and biology were enough. How things worked, not why, became primary, as naturalism moved from the fringes to common belief. Giving support to the growing focus on this world alone, naturalism added its voice to the chorus that either criticized Christianity or simply paid it no heed.

Kant's exhortation to "think boldly" pushed against repressing limits or boundaries to human thought.[59] However, even the best and brightest among us benefit from boundaries. If boundaries are no more than human constructs, then they are provisional and can be questioned, negotiated, and altered. But if some boundaries are patterns and laws given by God in creation, then recognizing their givenness is the first step in authentic thinking, even in bold thinking. Recognition of this givenness—of grace—is a discovery that in no way represses thought; to the contrary, it opens onto realistic and creative possibilities.

The choice of starting point is decisive: reason alone or faith seeking understanding. If we are the intended recipients of divine creation, then turning away from creation and attempting autonomy is a failure of thought, not its bold extension. To turn away from creation is to exercise freedom toward frustration. From the nineteenth to the twenty-first centuries, the turn toward reason alone, especially reason as the tool of criticism, has not led to expansion but to the fracturing of discourse. The critical, interrogative mood is not stable. It can function well as an intermediary en route to new stability, but criticism alone gives the mind neither rest nor accomplishment. In families, schools, and the wider society, the unrestrained practice of autonomy and criticism becomes socially destructive.

When he became rector of his university, Kant had to lead the academic procession to the chapel for religious services. Upon reaching the chapel Kant would step aside without entering. In an important sense, the Enlightenment itself took this kind of turn—away from the church, away from tradition, and toward the individual.

There is no problem in directing energetic attention to human affairs; but if we really do inhabit a divine creation, there is an enormous problem in attempting to shape human affairs without God. Cutting out the ultimate purpose of human life inevitably distorts lesser purposes, lifting lesser things to heights that they cannot sustain. A flawed view of eternity—or worse, the secular disregard of eternity—inevitably warps the transactions of time.

From the Age of Reason to Revolution: Unleashing the Furies

On a lovely May morning in 1789, in a festive procession to the Parisian Church of St. Louis, representatives of the Three Estates General—the clergy, aristocracy, and commoners—were followed by the king. Convened to address France's severe financial and political crisis, the Three Estates had not been assembled for about 175 years; as a result, traditions of shared governance and political problem-solving were little more than a faint historical memory.[60] In the heady days following the peaceful, almost exuberant beginning, a National Assembly was formed, a constitution was written, and the idealistic Declaration of the Rights of Man and of the Citizen was solemnly promulgated.[61] But as lines of authority began rapidly shifting, various zealous, extra-constitutional forces were formed, like the Paris Commune of Jacobins. At the hands of the Jacobins many of the clergy and the aristocracy would soon either be executed or in exile, the king and queen guillotined. The Revolution, the attempted fulfillment of the Enlightenment, first devolved into erratic power struggles, then degenerated into the Terror.

New Religion for a New Man

The recently concluded American Revolution had been primarily about self-governance; it was not anthropological, for it did not try to redefine what it means to be human. But the French Revolution was different: it began, as had the American, with issues of governance; but it quickly deepened and broadened into an attempt to reshape every aspect of human life—the church, dress and speech codes, street names, and even the calendar.

Seeking to reshape human life, revolutionary leaders drew upon Jean-Jacques Rousseau's renowned and widely revered *Social Contract*:

> He who dares to undertake the making of a people's institutions ought to feel himself capable . . . of changing human nature, of transforming each individual, who is by himself a complete and solitary whole, into part of a greater whole from which he in a manner receives his life and being; of altering man's constitution for the purpose of strengthening it.[62]

Rousseau's evocative exhortations are loaded with visionary aims—and tragic hubris. "To undertake the making of a people's institutions" is a massive endeavor; glibly to assume that this undertaking would also make someone "capable . . . of changing human nature, of transforming each individual" is Promethean arrogation. In relation to God the transformation of human character, being made in God's image and likeness, had long been an aim of Christian teaching. To leave God aside and declare that human leaders "ought to feel . . . capable" of directing such transformation is a recipe for catastrophe. But to add that the individual person is to be submerged "into part of a greater whole from which he in a manner receives his life and being" is to drain the cup of humanistic arrogance. Here again, leaving aside the belief that we receive "life and being" from God, the French Revolution would follow Rousseau. Like twentieth-century totalitarianisms, the Revolution tragically demanded individual submersion into the "greater whole," a lure of a humanist counterfeit of transcendence.

Deeply influenced by Rousseau, the Jacobin leader Maximilien de Robespierre applied the language of transcendence to the immanental aspirations and activities of the Revolution: "Which of us would care to descend from the heights of the *eternal principles* we have proclaimed to the actual government of [other] republics? . . . It is not enough to have overturned the throne; our concern is to erect upon its remains *holy Equality* and the *sacred* Rights of Man."[63] This invocation of what is "eternal," "holy," and "sacred" co-opts concepts previously associated with God and turns them toward the Revolution's objectives.

Every young person learning mechanical skills must become acquainted with how much weight a given material can bear, how tight a screw should go, or how pliant the material is. Too much weight, torque, or bending will result in cracking or breaking that can be hard to repair. In attempting to fuse revolution and religion, the French Revolution placed a spiritual weight on the nation that it could not bear. The ensuing disaster was far reaching.

Like Robespierre, the discourse of the Revolution commonly took transcendental religious terms and concepts and turned them to immanental political and economic purposes. It conscripted terms like "catechism," "creed," "gospel," "martyr," and "missionary" and sent them into the political battles of the fledgling republic.[64] The Catholic Church had long trained the French people in Christian symbols and concepts of transcendence. Leaders of the Revolution understood the power of symbols and the human need for believing in something greater than the self, and they redirected those symbols and concepts from God and the church to the state and its citizens. The Tree of Liberty replaced the Cross, the Reason of Man replaced divine grace, and the Revolution replaced and became its own kind of redemption.[65] That these replacements would cause such great sorrow, disruption, death, and destruction was theologically predictable.

A New Kind of Catechism

Revolutionary clubs became the churches of the new religion. Thus one Jacobin wrote a kind of instruction manual: "How was the Christian religion established? By the preaching of the apostles of the Gospel. How can we firmly establish the Constitution? By the mission of the apostles of liberty and equality."[66] This manual of religious exhortation then proceeded with practical advice on what each "apostle" should take along on the mission, such items as the Declaration of the Rights of Man, the Constitution, and a revolutionary almanac.

Attempting to obliterate the previous eighteen centuries of religious and political tradition, the Jacobins presented a new catechism:

> **Question**: What is Baptism?
>
> **Answer**: It is the regeneration of the French begun on 14 July 1789, and soon supported by the entire French nation.
>
> . . . .
>
> **Question**: What is Communion?
>
> **Answer**: It is the association proposed to all peoples by the French Republic henceforth to form on earth only one family of brothers who no longer recognise or worship any idol or tyrant.

> **Question**: What is Penitence?
>
> **Answer**: Today it is the wandering existence of traitors to their Fatherland. It is the banishment of all those monsters who, unworthy to inhabit the land of Liberty and to share the benefits which their villainy has only delayed, will soon be driven out of every corner of the globe, and having become an abomination to all life, will have no refuge except in the bowels of the earth which they have overly polluted with their crimes.[67]

This catechism calls for adoration of the Fatherland, not "Our Father"; it calls for the expulsion and death of dissenters, not for their instruction and love. Drawing upon Rousseau's *Social Contract*, Robespierre declared in 1792, "The soul of the Republic is virtue, it's the love of the fatherland, the magnanimous devotion which subsumes all particular interests in the general one."[68] Here again Christianity is to be replaced by a national religion—the humanistic immanental is to replace the divine transcendent. There is "one family of brothers," but those brothers who do not recognize the sovereign Fatherland, the revolutionary state, are brothers who must die.

The State Controls the Church

All over Europe the ancien régime was characterized by close relationships of church and state, and relations between the Gallican church and state were so intertwined that a major disruption to the state could not help but affect the church. Revolt against the state virtually guaranteed revolt against the church.

Given the historical linkage of church and state, it is not surprising that the revolutionary state would attempt to reconfigure that relationship—whatever sincerity or utter pretense was involved.[69] What is clear is that in late 1789, when the National Assembly was confronting a severe deficit in cash, it voted to confiscate church property. The properties taken from the church were sold for four hundred million livres to back the state's new paper money, the *assignats*. Bishops and priests were limited in power and put on modest salaries to be paid by the National Assembly.[70] Charitably seen, these seizures of church authority and property were attempts at reform; seen less charitably, they were attempts to destroy the church.[71]

But the encroachments went further. In February 1790 monasteries and convents not engaged in what the state deemed to be useful work were dissolved and forbidden to take new novices—an act with drastic ramifications for the future of the church. In 1792, when war broke out with Austria, church buildings were plundered for their precious metals and then for any metal that would help provide munitions for the war efforts.[72] Having reduced the church to financial dependence on the state, a new law was passed that bishops had to be elected by state officials in their departments and priests had to be elected by state officials in their district.[73] The Revolution was deeply serious about a new kind of religion—the service of the state.

As early as 1789, the Declaration of the Rights of Man had made explicit the state's power over the church: "The principle of all sovereignty resides essentially in the nation. No body nor individual may exercise any authority which does not proceed directly from the nation" (Article 3). The state then established a Civil Constitution of the Clergy that would have profoundly deleterious social, political, and spiritual results, not least of which would be religious schism. All clerics were required to swear an oath of fealty to the new Civil Constitution. Those who refused to swear, the non-juring priests and bishops, were deprived of their state-sanctioned status. Social and spiritual chaos followed when juring priests were hostilely received in their parishes.[74] The chaos further increased when the pope excommunicated priests who had sworn the oath and refused to recant.[75] The mingled presence of conflicting juring and non-juring priests added to the general chaos.[76] Devout parishioners did not want to take communion from juring priests who had been excommunicated.

The day after Louis XVI assented to the Civil Constitution, he received a letter from Pope Pius VI that condemned it.[77] Events were spinning out of control, so that major players had to think on their feet—and did not always do so very well. As in any massive transformation, there were initially a variety of views. Ominously, the permitted range of views would soon narrow drastically, as the Revolution plunged into chaos, death, and disaster.

In a late but courageous act, King Louis XVI refused to agree to a second law against the non-juring priests. Perhaps cognizant of what would soon take place, he said, "I have finished with men. I must turn to God."[78]

Attack and Replace

The Revolution's animus toward Christianity was already lurking in two of its revered Enlightenment predecessors, Rousseau and Voltaire, whose earthly remains were reverently disinterred and transferred to the Pantheon with elaborate ceremonies and quasi-religious processions.[79] Voltaire's detestation of Christianity was well known. In a letter to Frederick the Great, Voltaire did not hide his contempt for Christian faith: "Your Majesty will do the human race an eternal service in extirpating this infamous superstition."[80] With Rousseau and Voltaire as revered saints and Robespierre as high priest, the new church of the Jacobin society (moving faster and farther than Robespierre thought wise) sought to replace Christianity, which many revolutionaries saw as a superstitious relic.

As the revolutionaries attempted to reengineer life from tip to toe, they produced a new calendar. But tragicomically, there was considerable debate about whether the first day and year should coincide with the fall of the Bastille on July 14, 1789, or a later date to mark the executions of the king and queen.[81] In either case, the beginning of the Revolution, not the birth of Christ, would be the new measure and ever-present reminder of the flow of time. Even streets were renamed, as were individuals. The efforts were far-flung; the goal was to remove every trace of the Christian tradition that had shaped France and its people, to forge a new France and a new kind of human person.

Being made in the image and likeness of God would no longer suffice in the formation of self-identity. Instead, books of republican manners and morals attempted to inculcate a "new man" who would speak and act in a prescribed manner; and there were public ceremonies with civic homilies, readings of the Rights of Man, public oaths, and honors bestowed on some exemplary citizen. In the rapidly moving and turbulent events of the overhaul, new ideas were often put forth. Thus, for example, the Jacobin Louis de Saint-Just was an early advocate of socialism, which he deemed suitable for the new men in the new way of life.[82]

As the revolutionary overhaul proceeded, tolerance of its constitutionally controlled Catholicism began to disappear. During the winter of 1792 to 1793, a third of the French lower clergy and three-quarters of the bishops went into exile.[83] Those non-juring priests and bishops who remained in France had to hide, be disguised, and remain on the run. Before the Revolution, there were about 40,000 parishes; by 1794, only 150 parishes were openly celebrating mass.[84] Earlier attempts at cooperation between church and state degenerated into the Revolution's mode of attack and replace. Joseph Fouché announced that it was necessary "to substitute the worship of the Republic and natural morality for the superstitious cults to which the people still unfortunately adhere." Promoting his mission through mockery, Fouché put on a public anti-Christian show in Lyon, during which a donkey wore a bishop's cope and miter while it dragged a missal and the Gospels through the streets.[85] Something very different from the Christian hymns publicly sung at the Revolution's beginning was now underway.

In a highly symbolic event on November 10, 1793, the attack-and-replace efforts went much further: a revolutionary ceremony converted Notre Dame Cathedral into the Temple of Reason. Inside the cathedral, a mountain (a Jacobin symbol) was constructed at the nave and at the base was a plaque dedicated to reason; outside, the slogan of the republic, *Liberté, Egalité, Fraternité*, was chiseled onto one of the cathedral's stones. The attempt to replace Christianity was in full steam.

For Robespierre, the Revolution was a sacred beginning, a heroic first step in the forward march of progress, and progress was a common revolutionary motive for moving past Christianity. As historian Christopher Dawson notes, Robespierre saw the Revolution as "the birth of a new moral world and the regeneration of humanity."[86] Unlike Robespierre, who retained some form of belief in a Supreme Being, Anacharsis Cloots looked for progress that did away with any trace of a transcendent being. No longer looking beyond humanity, Cloots professed atheism regarding God and faith regarding humanity—the humanity found in the new France: "The attributes of an imaginary god truly belong to a divine politics. . . . The human race is God and only the aristocrats are atheists."[87] Holding progress as the highest reality, revolutionary leaders and their international sympathizers did not lack in self-confidence. Thus Giuseppe Cerutti declared "that they had destroyed fourteen centuries of abuses in three years, that the Constitution they had made would endure for centuries, and that their names would be blessed by future generations."[88] Like the later Thousand Year Reich in Germany that would last twelve years, what was supposed to endure for centuries in France would also last about twelve years, with the names of its leaders anything but blessed.

Progress in human affairs is not antithetical to Christian faith.[89] Ironically, looking to the affairs of eternity serves human affairs by placing the quest for progress in a greater, more valuable, and more enduring context. Human affairs are of great value, but they are not of ultimate value. Placing ultimate concerns onto something that cannot bear the weight is a doomed enterprise, no matter how many times it is tried.

Brotherhood Turns to Terror

Guided by its motto of "Liberty, Equality, and Fraternity," the Revolution began with a lofty vision of human rights and brotherhood. But as it attempted to implement its Enlightenment ideals, its sweeping endeavors degenerated into the bloodshed of the Terror, its mass killings foreshadowing the totalitarian horrors of the twentieth century.

Spiritually inebriated by the belief that they stood at the apex of human history, revolutionary leaders attempted to revamp the beliefs and behavior of the entire nation, and even the world. In just six years of the Revolution, successive French assemblies passed 15,479 laws.[90] The sheer impossibility of even knowing all the laws, let alone complying with them, indicates the frenetic nature of the revamping. It is not just that they attempted to do too much too quickly; what they attempted was also terribly wrong. Despite at first appearing to tolerate Christianity, the totalitarianism of the revolutionary vision eventually made inevitable the attempt to de-Christianize the populace.

On January 21, 1793, the king was guillotined; nine months later the queen shared his fate. Like a ricocheting projectile, power swung from the Assembly to the Convention to the unelected Paris Commune, with the extremist Jacobins Georges-Jacques Danton, Jean-Paul Marat, and Robespierre forming an unofficial triumvirate.[91] Whatever the noble aspirations in the Declaration, with its talk of being "under the auspices of the Supreme Being" and articulating the "rights of Man and of the Citizen," citizens who fell afoul of whoever happened to be in charge were summarily executed.

In spite of the dangers, resistance to Jacobin rule was attempted by the people of the Vendée and adjacent areas who objected to the Revolution's de-Christianizing practices. After the execution of the king, non-juring priests were sentenced to execution. However, the Vendéens were enraged when their non-juring priests were removed and replaced by those who had sworn fealty to the republic. Having recently undergone a religious revival similar to that of Methodism in England, the people of the Vendée were not willing to let their faith be overruled by revolutionary dictates. These poorly armed citizens at first succeeded against the well-equipped, more professional armies of the republic, but eventually they were crushed, some 250,000 losing their lives. Revolutionary *Fraternité* had now descended into warfare and mass slaughter, with thousands preferring death to yielding their faith.[92] As many as one-third of the population of the Vendée perished in the mass extermination—an eighteenth-century atrocity and omen of things to come.

As France faced attacks from other European powers and insurrection in the Vendée, Robespierre emulated Rousseau's "general will" as he forebodingly declared, "A single will is necessary."[93] The art form of civility, including disagreeing peacefully, cannot be practiced in totalitarian contexts and cannot be practiced when "a single will is necessary." The last six months of 1793 sank into the depths of the Terror, with despotic, dictatorial powers asserted by the so-called Committee of Public Safety and the Committee of General Security, who exerted their will on every aspect of public and private life. As Robespierre's associate Saint-Just menacingly declared, "You have to punish not only the traitors but also the indifferent; you have to punish whoever is passive in the Republic and does nothing for it. . . . Those who cannot be ruled by justice must be ruled by the sword."[94] Much like the later Bolsheviks in Russia, these Jacobins justified extreme measures as preparation for a later realm of constitutional governance and peace, a realm that never would arrive.

During the last three months of the Terror, the Jacobins managed to execute France's greatest scientist, Antoine Lavoisier; the poet André Chénier; and Madame Elisabeth, a woman of great faith and fortitude, widely loved and respected, and the youngest sibling of Louis XVI. Almost unspeakably, they also executed sixteen Carmelite nuns, who preferred death to giving up their vows to Christ. With remarkable courage, these women sang hymns and offered prayers at the foot of the guillotine. Before each one ascended, she would ask the prioress, "Permission to die, Mother?" to which the prioress responded, "Go, my daughter!" After her fifteen daughters had been beheaded, the prioress Madame Lidoine ascended the steps for her own martyrdom.[95] The fanatical barbarity of the Revolution was now unmistakably clear; the utopian dream had become an evil actuality.

The twisted irony to the execution of the Carmelites and so many other priests, bishops, and laypeople is laid out in a central document of the revolutionary "catechism," the Declaration of the Rights of Man: "The aim of all political association is the preservation of the natural and imprescriptible rights of man. These rights are liberty, property, security, and resistance to oppression" (Article 2). And yet the darkness of oppression had a silver lining: persecution winnowed out those not wholly committed to Christ, and it highlighted the faith and courage of those who were.

The murderous storm came to something of an end with the deaths of Robespierre and Saint-Just, who were themselves guillotined when the perceived power suddenly slipped away from them. The Jacobins were speedily rounded up, tried, and condemned. As if the country wished to catch its breath, some degree of mercy and civility returned:

priests were permitted to function; Vendéens were exempted from military service and even granted some payment for their losses; and religious liberty was generally restored.[96]

After the Terror and subsequent Napoleonic Wars had spent their dark energies, a religious revival occurred in both Catholic and Protestant countries. The church had lost property and privileges, not to mention hundreds of priests and bishops; but the courage of priestly martyrs greatly increased the esteem in which clergy were held. When, for example, Abbé Pinot mounted the scaffold for his execution, he intoned the well-known opening words of the mass: "I will go up to the altar of God" (*Introibo ad altare Dei*).[97] As Tertullian had centuries before proclaimed against Roman oppression, "The blood of Christians is seed."[98]

Given the lofty nature of their task, priests and ministers must be good shepherds who are willing, if called to do so, to lay down their lives for the flock. There is a human hunger for good leadership, and a strong response typically follows its appearance. Clergy who had risked their lives offering mass in secret and those who had been martyred were later held in very high regard. The rebound result of oppression was renewed religious devotion.

• • •

Looking at the French Revolution through a theological lens, we can appreciate some of the noble aspirations with which it began, yet lament the murderous, totalitarian attack on the church into which it fell. There is a human tendency to error, evil, and sin whose counterweight is the gospel of Christ. But the Declaration of the Rights of Man claimed to have found a different source of evil, "believing that the ignorance, neglect, or contempt of the rights of man are the sole cause of public calamities and of the corruption of governments." What is at stake is highlighted by juxtaposing the Christian warning about the human capacity for evil with the Revolution's overweening confidence—and the devastation that it brought. The French had greatly admired the American Revolution; but where the American Revolution was bolstered by its people's faith, the French Revolution became the persecutor of faith. Leaving all humility aside, extreme ideologies, being blind to human frailty and evil, tend toward calamity. As the Hebrew writer long ago warned, "Pride goes before destruction, and a haughty spirit before a fall" (Prov 16:18).

The French Revolution veered from recognizing a transcendent God to elevating the immanental and exclusively human, and then persecuting, attacking, and attempting to replace Christianity. In Arnold Toynbee's assessment, the Revolution displayed "the fanatical worship of collective human power."[99] It was a harbinger of Leninist-Stalinist, Maoist, and Hitlerian things to come.

The quest for human brotherhood was undoubtedly (at least in the beginning) as sincere as it was doomed. Visions of human brotherhood without God's fatherhood are predictable failures, as they were in France and would be in the later Russian Revolution.

With its Promethean principles placing all responsibility in human hands, the French Revolution was the epitome of overreach. As historian Richard Crane puts it, "The dream of republican democracy was short-lived, drowned in blood in its first two years, compromised by a corrupt oligarchy for its next half-decade, and stifled by a military dictator in its last five twilight years."[100] The failures of the French Revolution and the later Russian Revolution point to a fundamental choice: either humanity exists because of God, for relationship with God, as the human family of God; or humanity is on its own, free to carve out its own meaning in an otherwise meaningless universe.

• • •

Our theological narrative has examined the critical turns of the Reformation, Enlightenment, and French Revolution. As these historical movements pried open new pathways, they progressively shattered old foundations. Theologically assessing the grand sweep of this history has afforded a glimpse of the historical roots of our own pressing religious problems. We live in the mélange of what they achieved and what they shattered.

As the Enlightenment and French Revolution turned toward solely humanistic concerns, the religion spawned by the incarnation of the Son of God was variously ignored, critiqued, or viciously attacked. If Reimarus and Strauss had been right in contending that incarnation is merely fraud or myth, then an exclusive humanism really would be the most truthful response, the best that we could do. But if the incarnation and its events are the intersection of divine and human, and the turning point of human history, then it is no small thing to turn away from them, or worse, to attack a divine gift that included the cost of crucifixion.

Paul Valéry once noted that "civilizations are mortal."[101] Because nations and empires are mortal, faith in even the best of human civilizations and governments is badly misdirected. The hope of eternity is foolishly placed on the ephemeral forms of human civilization and governance. Civilizations are indeed mortal, as is each human person. But we are mortals to whom Christ has promised immortality. The promise cannot be proved, only believed. But there are inklings, hints, and, for countless many, confirmations of the highest predilections of the human heart. Thus when the prophet Isaiah witnessed the fall of the Babylonian Empire, with its unexpected liberation of the Jewish people, he proclaimed an insight for the citizens of all ages: "The grass withers, the flower fades; but the word of our God will stand forever" (Isa 40:8).

2
DESCENT INTO DARKNESS
Romanticism, Atheism, Nihilism, Marxism

> The superhuman God is only imaginary, an edifying cliché, and a toy of fantasy. . . . God, as we conceive and think him, is our ego, our mind, and our essence; but this God is only an appearance of us and for us, not God in himself.
>
> **Ludwig Feuerbach**

> Tyrannical toward himself, he must be tyrannical toward others. All the gentle and enervating sentiments of kinship, love, friendship, gratitude, and even honor, must be suppressed in him and give place to the cold and single-minded passion for revolution. . . . Night and day he must have but one thought, one aim—merciless destruction. Striving cold-bloodedly and indefatigably toward this end, he must be prepared to destroy himself and to destroy with his own hands everything that stands in the path of the revolution.
>
> **Sergei Nechaev**

> Repudiate Christ and the human mind can arrive at the most astonishing conclusions.
>
> **Fyodor Dostoevsky**[1]

Having at first inspired exuberance and hope, the French Revolution was avidly followed across Europe. But when the Revolution careened into the Terror and subsequent Napoleonic Wars, the shock and disappointment were widespread. In 1807, Samuel Taylor Coleridge poetically captured Europe's emotional swings about the Revolution—soaring expectation followed by dismal letdown:

> When from the general heart of humankind
> Hope sprang forth like a full-born Deity!
> —Of that dear Hope afflicted and struck down . . .[2]

The ebullient hope was that the Revolution, its energy drawn not from divine transcendence but from liberated human possibility, would be the apotheosis of the Enlightenment, a glorious new epoch springing forth "from the general heart of humankind." But when the Revolution came to grief, its hope "afflicted and struck down," there was understandably some confusion in religious, political, and social domains. With previous certainties shattered and with the Revolution's demise, old traditions continued as new movements pulled in different directions, some of them dangerous and deadly.

The situation was complex. It included ongoing expressions of Christian and Jewish faith, a growing number of Masons and Rosicrucians, lingering Enlightenment attempts at morality, calls for benevolence and love, and various other attempts to improve human life. But the nineteenth century also saw a strange descent into darkness, the primary focus of this current chapter.

In large part the Enlightenment had been launched as a rationalist critique of Christianity. But in the Romantic movement, men and women increasingly came forth who rejected both Christian faith *and* the Enlightenment.[3] The Enlightenment quest for reason was not so much attacked as just left aside. To a growing number of artists, novelists, poets, and musicians, the rule of reason seemed too restrictive. Bucking against moral imperatives and universal reason, the Romantic movement turned inward to the liberation of individual passion, to the primacy of feeling. Some decades earlier Jean-Jacques Rousseau had already declared, "Provided that you *feel* that I am right, I do not bother to prove it to you."[4] As the Romantic movement unfolded, the constrained artistry of Franz Joseph Haydn gave way to the outburst artistry of Ludwig van Beethoven; freedom of expression struggled against externally imposed form.

The Romantic period was a many-sided philosophic and artistic movement that could draw upon Christian thought and biblical texts without being committed to them. Christian imagery was diverted from a believed-in God and sequestered to elevate the liberated ego. Just as Christianity draws its power by looking to something infinite and eternal, so too did eminent writers like Johann Wolfgang von Goethe and George Gordon Lord Byron look for something surpassing and unlimited, but only to express passion with preternatural intensity. To spur their narratives onto new heights, Goethe, Byron, and others created heroes like Faust and Manfred who audaciously tapped the energy of the demonic. According to Michael Gillespie,

> Demonic names a dark and powerful but essentially negative will underlying the phenomena, a will that may arise out of the divine but is opposed to it, and that empowers and liberates certain individuals but also catapults them beyond the bounds of conventional morality into what is simultaneously an exalted state of superhumanity and a degraded state of bestiality. They are rebels against God and are willing to accept whatever penalty he exacts, unafraid, doing what they will, taking what they will, destroyers, conquerors, revolutionaries.[5]

Demonically catapulted beyond social and moral boundaries, these fictional heroes modeled the expansion and glorification of the ego—the untrammeled will of the individual.

Yet as we shall see, alongside and in some ways crisscrossing with Romantic excess arose Ludwig Feuerbach's philosophical argument for atheism coupled with advocacy of human love. Further complicating matters was the rise of nihilism—the utterly skeptical belief that nothing mattered. This extreme skepticism, which we will examine in Ivan Turgenev's *Fathers and Sons*, denied the very possibility of truth, goodness, and meaning in human life.

This spiritually depressed topography also gave rise to Marxism—a new kind of revolutionary fervor that starkly differed from the optimistic origins of the French and American revolutions. From the outset Marxism, like nihilism and anarchism, was colder, harder, angrier; and it would prove to be deadlier. Believing life to be entirely material, Marxists initiated social and political movements whose protean toxins have never gone away—toxins which continue to globally infest educational, political, and religious institutions.

By the mid-nineteenth century, the most basic orientations were no longer binary choices, no longer Christian faith versus atheism, reason versus superstition, monarchy versus democracy. How to go about life was no longer an inherited expectation, but a choice among multiple options. Friedrich Nietzsche, claiming "that the Christian God has ceased to be believable," found the situation exhilarating: "At last our ships may venture out again, venture out to face any danger; . . . the sea, *our* sea, lies open again; perhaps there has never yet been such an 'open sea.'"[6] While we may agree that the time was exciting, for the health of all aboard, and for the future of the vessel, ships at sea generally do require a destination. But to ask about a destination is to raise the fundamental issue: Is humankind en route to an already given destination, or are we simply to set out upon an open but ultimately meaningless sea?

In what follows, our theological task is to trace the historical roots of twenty-first century problems by encountering what certain seminal figures of the nineteenth century (and early twentieth century) wrote and wrought: the celebration of the unhindered ego, atheism, nihilism, anarchism, and Marxism. Rather different from a happy outing on an "open sea," these exclusively humanist endeavors have proved to be far from innocent, bringing human misery on a colossal scale. Looking closely at these philosophical, literary, and political departures from Christian faith, our purpose is to see these forays into darkness for what they always have been—and to counteract their lingering spell with "light kindled from the Gospel."[7]

A Philosophical Turning Point: Atheism Unfurled

Once philosophy ceased being the handmaid of theology (*ancilla theologiae*), philosophers began to present independent views about God, the world, and humanity. From among the many eminent nineteenth-century philosophers, Ludwig Feuerbach (1804–1872) plays a crucial role for our narrative through his open embrace of atheism. Where biblical scholar David Friedrich Strauss argued that Jesus' divinity was an historical illusion, Feuerbach went farther, arguing that the very existence of God was a psychological illusion.[8] After Feuerbach, philosophers, novelists, and a new breed of political revolutionaries would thematically focus on this world alone. Many leaders of the communist movement saw Feuerbach as their intellectual and spiritual father. That ideas affect behaviors is especially clear in the influence of this philosopher and anti-theologian.

Feuerbach argued that thinking about God is the highest potential of human thought. When we think about God, however, we are actually thinking about ourselves, because God is a creation of the human mind: "God, as we conceive and think of him, is our ego, our mind, and our essence."[9] We should think God; it is essential that we think God, because such thinking elevates our thought. But apart from the highest reaches of the human mind, we should not think that God exists. In stretching the human mind toward its highest potential, transcendence is a noble goal, but ultimately, transcendence is a chimera of immanence: "The new philosophy is the complete and absolute dissolution . . . of theology into anthropology."[10] With this publicly declared atheism the West's critical turn reached its terminus: God does not exist; everything falls on human shoulders.

Feuerbach knew Christian doctrine well, and in partial agreement with Jesus' love commands (Mark 12:28-31), Feuerbach thought that loving others, even loving all people, was crucial: "Love is objectively as well as subjectively the criterion of being, of truth, and of reality. Where there is no love, there is also no truth. And only he who loves something is something."[11]

Like earlier Enlightenment thinkers, Feuerbach advocated for morality, not because a god had commanded it, but because morality is good for humanity. Wishing to avoid egocentricity, he called for each one to achieve virtue by participating in divinity through love. From Spinoza to Feuerbach to our own time, the myth of the virtuous atheist has become increasingly well established.

Feuerbach's morality without God, his exclusive humanism, greatly influenced political writers and activists like Friedrich Engels, Karl Marx, Sergei Nechaev, Mikhail Bakunin, and Vladimir Lenin, and fiction writers like Ivan Turgenev and Nikolay Chernyshevsky. Marx, for example, echoed Feuerbach in declaring, "The religion of the workers has no god, because it seeks to restore the divinity of man."[12] Feuerbach held community in the highest regard: "The essence of man is contained only in the community and unity of man with man."[13] However, having discarded the heavenly Father that would have grounded the corollary of human brotherhood, it was just a step further to discard the brotherhood. Loving others was Feuerbach's stated preference; other preferences would soon be enacted.

Literary Intensifications

Portrayals of wondrous self-assertion were publicly disseminated in literature—the cutting-edge art form of the time. A large reading public for newspapers, pamphlets, poems, plays, and novels was an historic development that made human life more interesting. But reading was also a social accelerant: it made far more of the population aware of and concerned about decision-making that affected them—and also got the public concerned about much that did not directly affect them. Mass dissemination democratized the evolution of ideas, with multiple effects: it informed, instructed, entertained, and uplifted; but it could also degrade and propagandize.

In 1455, Johann Gutenberg's invention of the printing press had fostered translations of the Bible into commonly spoken languages like English, French, and German. Once these translations were available, because people wanted to be able to read the Bible, literacy greatly increased. Similarly, during the eighteenth century, the production of encyclopedias spread Enlightenment ideals and general knowledge to ever larger numbers of people. The printed word, which could be used for truth or falsehood, good or evil, beauty or ugliness, added democratized complexity to the fabric of civilization.[14]

In addition to and sometimes in mutual influence with philosophers, Romantic writers took bold new paths of expressive poetry and fiction. One of the foremost was William Blake (1757–1827), whose immensely popular poem "The Tyger" (1794) encapsulated the allurement, the mesmerizing attraction of the deadly and destructive. And most importantly, the poem asks about the Creator-source of the killer tiger:

> Did he smile his work to see?
> Did he who made the Lamb make thee?

Coupling beauty and merciless destruction, the tiger leads us to question why creation includes tigers as well as lambs. With its symmetrical markings and latent power, its menacing eyes punctuating the night of the jungle, the tiger lives by strength. It does not and cannot pity weakness. Blake's questions were provocative:

> What immortal hand or eye,
> Could frame thy fearful symmetry?
>
> In what distant deeps or skies.
> Burnt the fire of thine eyes?
> On what wings dare he aspire?
> What the hand, dare seize the fire?
>
> And what shoulder, & what art,
> Could twist the sinews of thy heart?
> . . . .
> What the hammer? what the chain,
> In what furnace was thy brain?
> What the anvil? what dread grasp,
> Dare its deadly terrors clasp!

Blake's "Tyger" was an invitation to ponder the darker, more menacing side of creation. To imitate the tiger's Creator, to "dare seize the fire," would require strong and skillful hands. As if Blake had laid out a challenge—"What the anvil? what dread grasp, / Dare its deadly terrors clasp!"—numerous souls accepted the dare to attempt the "dread grasp."

Both daring and duly renowned, Johann Wolfgang Goethe (1749–1832) pushed hard against the envelope of social norms. Goethe's *Faust* is a diabolically assisted plunge into unbounded feeling and action. As part of a wager through which he seeks Faust's soul, Mephistopheles promises Faust more for his senses in one hour than he could otherwise obtain in an entire year of monotony.[15] He offers him pleasure without limit: "To you no goal is set, nor measure. . . . May all agree with you that gives you pleasure!" (l. 1760, 1763). Typical of a Romantic hero, Faust seeks superhuman experience in this world alone. Seizing the innocent Gretchen's trembling hands, Faust declares,

> Let this hand-pressure say to you
> What is unspeakable:
> To give oneself up wholly and to feel
> A rapture that must be eternal!
> Eternal!—for its end would be despair.
> No! no end! No end! (l. 3189–94)

Stretching beyond the possible, communicating the "unspeakable," and retaining the intensity of feeling *eternally* are the desiderata of Romanticism—feelings and experiences that exceed human norms and limits. Pulling Gretchen into these diabolically empowered feelings and experiences, Faust promises her eternal rapture, but she is soon the picture of misery—alone in prison, bereft of mother, brother, and (Faust's) child whom she has drowned in a fit of madness—and sentenced to execution at morning's first light.

Romantic heroes are not the sort who marry, have children, and, over decades of work and developed relationships, contribute steadily to a community. Instead, the hero must be larger than life—and leave it while at his youthful height.[16] Early death is the fitting end point of wild and extreme passion.

In *Faust* Goethe embraces the diabolical but refuses to let it triumph. Despite Mephistopheles' desires, he ultimately (and unwillingly) serves the good. Goethe questionably maintained that even the demonic is ultimately good, because even demons are dependent on God. Thus, in spite of Faust's compact with the devil, in which Faust had wagered his own soul, a descending troupe of angels delivers Faust from Mephistopheles and to salvation. That both Gretchen (end of Part One) and Faust himself (end of Part Two) were given salvation displeased many of Goethe's contemporaries; but as ad hoc or even absurd as their fate seems, the ultimate triumph of good over evil was central to Goethe's worldview. Given his universal renown, his metaphysical principle that evil must serve the good served as a temporary brake upon the nihilistic tendency of the time. In pursuit of egoist passion, Faust's flirtation with the devil leads to acts of perjury, seduction, and murder; yet in spite of such extreme evil, the good is portrayed as more fundamental.[17] Goethe looks long and hard at the *nihil*, but he ends by stepping away from it.

In addition to the unlikely salvation of two of the central characters, it is striking that Goethe even retained the notion of salvation. From beginning to end, *Faust* is saturated with allusions to scripture and Christian tradition. The power of Christianity is the base from which the tale is told and turned. Thus a prologue in Heaven precedes Part One, whose resemblance to the prologue in the biblical book of Job is unmistakable, both works being largely based on a bet between the Lord and Satan or Mephistopheles. Old and New Testament references abound; Faust first encounters Gretchen just after she is returning from confession (where she has nothing to confess); angels, demons, and God are crucial to the story.

In a work bearing strong similarity to *Faust*, Ludwig Tieck's *William Lovell* (1796) presented a demonic hero who rejects all convention and morality as he subjects all around him to himself.[18] The eponymous William Lovell and Faust both behave in egregious ways. Just as Lovell seduces an innocent peasant girl, Faust seduces the innocent and pure-of-heart Gretchen. Lovell murders his peasant girl's fiancé; Faust kills Gretchen's brother in a duel. Lovell abandons his peasant lover; Faust abandons Gretchen while she is pregnant. After poisoning his best friend, Lovell seduces and abducts his sister; Faust cannot harm his best friend, because Faust has no friends. But Faust's dalliance with the devil does manage to get several innocent people killed. The point of these behaviors is not merely to violate social norms; rather, it is to express the feelings and desires of the unhindered ego. Those who remain under the moral law of their society, those who refuse the force of demonic power, cannot ignite the blaze of unlimited self-expression. The Romantic hero does not seek to harm others, although he typically does so. Faust, for example, is deeply grieved by Gretchen's sorry state. It is rather the case that the hero cannot be fenced in by social mores or by others' interests; the will must be asserted; sensual desires must be fulfilled—not merely for animalistic pleasures, but because striving to fulfill sexual pleasure is a method of liberating the full potential of the I. Demonic knowledge and power are denied to those restrained by social custom and moral law. To penetrate the depths of this world, to actualize the latent power of the I, one follows the tiger who dominates the world, not the lamb who takes away its sins.

What Goethe resisted doing in *Faust*, Lord Byron (1788–1824) fully indulged in his poem *Manfred*, a work that became a sensation in Europe.[19] Dressing darkness in noble gentility, the poem (1817) alludes to but does not portray Manfred's incest with his beautiful, gentle twin sister, which apparently led to her suicide. The three-act poem portrays untrammeled assertion of the will, conjuring of demonic spirits, and explicit refusal of grace and repentance. Manfred's incest with his *twin* sister is the perfect violation: the pursuit of superhuman ego must violate the most basic social and moral prohibitions en route to engulfing and devouring otherness. As Gillespie puts it, "The character of Manfred's crime is not accidental. It is the utmost expression of his being, the denial of otherness, the attempt to eliminate all boundaries and convert everything into the I."[20] His twin sister, whom he loves but destroys, is pointedly gentler and tenderer; like Blake's tiger, Manfred's boundless self must overtake and consume.

Unlike Kant's sense of autonomy, in *Manfred* autonomy is not limited by reason or anything else; autonomy is self-assertion of the will alone. Manfred denies all authority other than the self. When he conjures spirits to assist him converse with his deceased sister, he declares them his servants, not his master. He rejects the elderly Abbot's kind offer of the church's grace, of "penitence and pardon," and the Abbot's personal wish of redirecting Manfred to "higher hope and better thoughts" (III.i.57–62). And, most forcefully, on the verge of death Manfred confronts the demons come to transport him to hell: "I knew, and know my hour is come, but not / To render up my soul to such as thee" (III.iv.88–89). This third denial of external authority is striking in its mimicry of Jesus' words: "The hour has come for the Son of Man to be glorified" (John 12:23). As is so often the case, Romantic writers echo biblical teaching while turning the venerable phraseology to their own, distinctly nonreligious purpose.

For this world and for whatever is in the next, Manfred gives his own will supreme reign. He contemptuously wards off the demons:

> *Thou* didst not tempt me, and thou couldst not tempt me;
> I have not been thy dupe, nor am thy prey—
> But was my own destroyer, and will be
> My own hereafter.—Back, ye baffled fiends!—
> The hand of death is on me—but not yours! (III.iv.137–141)

Having heard Manfred's bold argument and command, the demons disappear. Manfred's tale, his heroic self-assertion and audacity, is the terminus of the Romantic self, the point beyond which there is only the nothingness of death or, perhaps, superhuman beings not in the least subject to human argument or willfulness.

It is crucial to Romantic artistry to keep characters like Manfred and Faust from simply being dismissed as villains. Thus Manfred is tormented by what he has done to his sister, although he never repents the act and would do it again. When Manfred meets a hunter on the mountain, the righteous but lowborn hunter duly sees Manfred's "cautious feeling for another's pain," and he doubts that Manfred could "be black with evil," noticing that Manfred is "one of gentle thoughts" and unlikely to have been a man of revenge (II.80–82). Manfred replies that he has always been fair to enemies; he has only injured those whom he has loved best (II.85–86). His winsome speech and gracious manner are likewise affirmed by the Abbot, the priest who seeks him out while Manfred is waiting for the devil and death. Thus the Abbot says of him,

> This should have been a noble creature: he
> Hath all the energy which would have made
> A goodly frame of glorious elements,
> Had they been wisely mingled. (III.1.160–63)

Faust is likewise tormented at Gretchen's disgrace, and he asks that all blame be heaped upon him, that Gretchen may die quickly, and that "her fate plunge crushing down on me!" (l. 3364). And both Manfred and Faust manifest strength against their various evil spirits, and they manifestly dislike them. Through this kind of artifice, characters otherwise unlikely to gain sympathy manage to do so.

In strong contrast to Byron, Jane Austen's *Pride and Prejudice* (1813), published just four years before *Manfred*, expressed a synthesis—Enlightenment dedication to morality, character development, and ordered eros—with ongoing allegiance to Christian faith (church is attended without being emphasized). Austen affirmed what Romantics in general and *Manfred* in particular denied: the value of limits. It was a Romantic commonplace for the portrayed hero to violate limits, especially in regard to sexual behavior and in pursuit of unmitigated feeling, assisted by forbidden commerce with dark, supernatural beings. Thus Mephistopheles' promise to Faust is a case in point: "To you no goal is set, nor measure" (l. 1760). But from a Christian perspective of creation, the limits of natural laws are divinely given for the good of the individual and the good of all people. By faith, the unlimited and infinite are incrementally available to the sons and daughters of God—but not of our will and making, and not in ruinous excess of human capacities. The impatient fire of the Romantic hero attempts to eliminate the natural limits and required pacings of time. But those who recognize the beauty and value of limits can look to a transcendent realm and Person whose imposed limits stem from infinite love, a limitless love that draws us to respect the given patterns of nature and to admire, respect, love, and serve others—not to engulf them in the unbounded desires of our own ego.

Austen's and Byron's publications display the competing vectors of the era. Old allegiances continued, like Austen's to the ordered ideals of the Enlightenment and of Christianity; and going in a very different direction, heroes like Manfred emerged with a less beneficent end—the unrestricted expression of the self.

Because so many were attracted by the myth of the unlimited self, widely read works of demonic egoism, especially in sexual relations, extended the borders of public discourse, thought, and behavior by colorful glamorizations of evil. In our own day, a segment of popular culture has progressively transgressed boundaries in ways that often make emancipation, titillation, and degradation indistinguishable, and in crossing boundaries expresses an underlying nihilism.

Fathers and Sons: A Narrative of Nihilism

According to Thomas Seltzer, "No event in the literary history of Russia ever created such a stir as the publication of Turgenev's *Fathers and Sons*."[21] When first published in 1862, the deeply skeptical main character Bazarov became a topic of national debate; and through this fictional character, Russian society was introduced to the term and the concept of nihilism.[22] The novel portrayed a chasm between the progressive, liberal generation of the enlightened fathers and the nihilism of the university-educated sons, and it undoubtedly broadened that chasm.

Enlightenment liberalism is portrayed as pathetic and passé, unable to transmit its values across generations, unable to hold its ground. The depth and consistency of Bazarov's nihilism seemed insane to the older characters, but Bazarov became a household name in Russia, and his kind of view would profoundly affect Russian government and society. The humanism of the Enlightenment and Romanticism had in some ways made the world more interesting, but the nihilistic sons were already bored with the world.

Nihilism: The Negation of Meaning

After completing university, Arkady is affectionately welcomed home, bringing with him his admired companion and would-be friend Bazarov. Arkady's first substantive conversation with his father and uncle becomes confrontational, as Arkady describes himself as a follower of Bazarov, who is off collecting samples for his study of nature. Arkady's uncle, the suave Pavel Petrovitch, has already been put off by Bazarov's lack of deference and by his strange ideas. With his suspicions aroused, Pavel pointedly asks his nephew, "What is Mr. Bazarov himself?" His nephew replies, "He's a nihilist." Noticing his uncle's puzzlement at the term, Arkady repeats, "He's a nihilist."

The term, unfamiliar to Arkady's father and uncle, was also unfamiliar to the Russian readership of 1862, but is now brought front and center, both as a philosophy and as a personal identity. Arkady's well-educated father muses aloud on what it means to be a nihilist. He says, "That's from the Latin, *nihil*, *nothing*, as far as I can judge; the word must mean a man who . . . who accepts nothing?" The uncle, his suspicions now confirmed, adds, "Say, 'who respects nothing.'" The son Arkady attempts an adjustment: "Who regards everything from the critical point of view." When Arkady's uncle asks, "Isn't that just the same thing?" Arkady claims that there is a difference: "A nihilist is a man who does not bow down before any authority, who does not take any principle on faith, whatever reverence that principle may be enshrined in." Tellingly, the uncle interrupts, "Well, and is that good?" Arkady refuses to recognize the universality of goodness: "That depends, uncle. Some people it will do good to, but some people will suffer for it."[23] Relativizing goodness and shrugging at any ensuing suffering bewilder the father and uncle. The older men understand the term "nihilism," but they do not understand why anyone would embrace it as a way of life.

This homecoming conversation between the father, uncle, and beloved son reveals a wide gap and portends danger—in the plot of the novel and in the Russian and world history about to unfold.

Nihilism and Naturalism

For Bazarov nature is only to be studied and mastered, not to be the source of poetic contemplation, let alone joy. When the aristocratic uncle Pavel is discussing various poets, Bazarov brusquely interrupts: "A good chemist is twenty times as useful as any poet." Asked if he denies all art and only believes in science, Bazarov denies even the belief in science: "I have already explained to you that I don't believe in anything." The nihilist is also an extreme naturalist; there are sciences, particular investigations of particular things, but not something abstract called "science." The leveling is all-encompassing; for the fathers, the gaping generational divide is highly unsettling.[24]

Arkady is dazzled by Bazarov but not as fully converted to his views as he believes himself to be. Pensively enjoying the beauty of the Russian countryside, Arkady asks, "And is nature foolery?" The fully converted Bazarov replies, "Nature, too, is foolery in the sense you understand it. Nature's not a temple, but a workshop, and man's the workman in it." The conversation ends in dissonant silence, as

Bazarov mockingly laughs upon hearing Arkady's father playing the cello, finding it ridiculous that a forty-four-year-old country gentleman would be interested in music.[25]

An Aroma of Christianity

Earlier, when Arkady's uncle Pavel—who never married—had an affair with a married princess and fell ardently in love with her, he asked to know her sphinxlike secret. When the Princess later broke off the relationship, she returned a ring to him with a pictorial message: the secret to her mysterious inner identity was the cross. Pavel gives no indication of disagreeing with the Princess' faith; such faith as he has is a more distant, less pressing concern.[26] If directly asked, Pavel and his brother would undoubtedly affirm Christian belief, just as they would confirm being Russian, just as they would uphold social decencies. But a diluted faith, one akin to good manners, is not sufficient to counter the nihilism thrust before them.

In a discussion among Uncle Pavel, Arkady, and Bazarov that becomes heated, Pavel's attempts to counter Bazarov have too weak a foundation. To no avail Pavel invokes character, personal dignity, the common good, the social fabric, and the aristocracy. Bazarov is not impressed: "Aristocracy, Liberalism, progress, principles, if you think of it, what a lot of foreign . . . and useless words!" Increasingly exasperated, Pavel responds, "If we listen to you, we shall find ourselves outside humanity, outside its laws."[27] When Pavel appeals to the logic of history, Bazarov denies its usefulness. All that is needed is a way to put bread in one's mouth; abstractions of every sort are useless. Bazarov is unflinchingly revealing the totality of his break from everything the older man holds dear when Pavel injects his challenging question, "Everything?" to which Bazarov unhesitatingly responds, "Everything." Both concerned and nonplussed, Pavel asks whether Bazarov rejects art, poetry, and "even . . . horrible to say . . ." Bazarov calmly gives him the unthinkable and unspeakable answer: "Everything."[28] We are left to infer that Bazarov and his fellow nihilists even reject faith in God.

Bazarov's offensive concepts are punctuated by the way he breaks off the debate, as though it also means nothing. When Pavel asks if Bazarov and Arkady will go on turning everything into ridicule, Bazarov scornfully responds, "No, will go on dissecting frogs. Come Arkady; goodbye for the present, gentlemen!"[29] The older men are left with the forlorn conclusion of how their heirs will handle the inheritance of their traditions: rupture rather than development is all they can expect.

Progress and Rupture

Some years after the death of his beloved wife, Arkady's father became intimate with his servant Fenitchka, who bore a son. Once aware of the situation, Arkady felt no ill will to his father or to Fenitchka; instead, he tells Bazarov that, in spite of their class difference, his father should marry the girl—Arkady thus displaying what he considered his admirably progressive attitude. Rather than applauding his progressivism, Bazarov disparages Arkady for being captive to an outworn principle: "You still attach significance to marriage; I did not expect that of you."[30] Bazarov is teaching his disciple and the Russian readership how extreme the leveling must be.

Arkady's father had done his best to do well by his peasants, to be open to the demands of progress; yet he recognizes that he is being left behind: "I try in every way to keep abreast with the requirements of the day—and they say my day's over. And, brother, I begin to think that it is."[31] He is a sympathetic figure who loves his son, loved his wife, and after her death, loved the lower-class Fenitchka. But to a nihilist, being progressive is as futile as being conservative, or being nothing at all.

Rupture with the past and dismissal of the future are reiterated by an acquaintance of the young nihilists, an emancipated woman who celebrates her childlessness: "Thank God, I'm independent: I've no children. . . . What was that I said: *thank God!* It's no matter though."[32] The utter lack of maternal feeling is suitably matched with the silliness of her self-reprimand for having referred to God in an old expression. As they imbibe a third and fourth bottle of champagne, they banter about whether marriage is a prejudice or a crime. That marriage might be something beautiful and worthwhile, a human privilege in creation, has receded beyond their horizon.

The nihilistic corrosion of family life is further dramatized when Bazarov knowingly and repeatedly disappoints his parents. After a three-year absence they are eagerly anticipating his homecoming, but he absents himself, even on the festive day of his guardian angel: "To-day they expect me home . . . . Well, they can go on expecting. . . . What does it matter!"[33] When Bazarov finally does return home, he stays only three days—leaving his devastated parents grieving in disbelief. Bazarov knows and in some sense appreciates that his parents love him, but familial affection is part of the value system from which he has decidedly broken off.

The Negation of Friendship and Romantic Love

After meeting the beautiful, highly intelligent, and regal Anna Sergyevna, Bazarov's observation shocks Arkady: "What a magnificent body. Shouldn't I like to see it on the dissecting table." Never quite the nihilist he aspires to be, Arkady exclaims, "Hush, for mercy's sake . . . that's beyond everything." Unrepentant, Bazarov responds, "Well, don't get angry, you baby. I meant it's first rate."[34] Equal parts youthful crassness and nihilist wittiness, Bazarov's objectifying comment is consistent with his view that taking material pleasure with women is acceptable—but not the eros of romantic love. Likewise, Bazarov and Arkady can be traveling companions and in some sense allies, but in Bazarov's scheme of things, friendship is not possible.

During a two-week visit at Anna's country estate, Bazarov and Anna, both very strong but in different ways, are increasingly drawn to one another. Anna had invited Arkady and Bazarov because, as she told Arkady, "I shall be very curious to see the man who has the courage to believe in nothing."[35] While Bazarov's radical views do not shock Anna, she expresses surprise that he has no artistic feeling, no poetic sense of nature, and no love of music. Bazarov goes further, denying the importance of individual persons:

> Studying separate individuals is not worth the trouble. All people are like one another, in soul as in body; each of us has brain, spleen, heart, and lungs made alike; and the so-called moral qualities are the same in all; the slight variations are of no importance. A single human specimen is sufficient to judge of all by. People are like trees in a forest; no botanist would think of studying each individual birch-tree.[36]

Bazarov's leveling speech is consistent with his worldview, but it is starkly inconsistent with what he and Anna are mutually experiencing: each is *only* interested in the other, fascinated by the other, and apart from all others, drawn to the other. Bazarov's relation with Anna is a lived, experienced contradiction to his philosophy.

The denial of each person's sacred particularity is crucial for nihilism, because the value of the *person* is a prerequisite for friendship and romantic love. If friendship and romantic love are authentic, the avowed nothingness would be negated. If friendship and love are real, the leveling of *everything* has failed: the set is no longer empty. In the light of friendship and love, the claim of nothingness becomes incoherent.

Hence, when Bazarov cannot keep himself from loving Anna, and when he declares such love to her, he most harshly judges his own feelings and inconsistent behavior. Bazarov scoffs at the idea of love, which he thought of as "lunacy, unpardonable imbecility; he regarded chivalrous sentiments as something of the nature of deformity or disease."[37] Bazarov was tortured by his inability to master his feelings of love for Anna. It seems that the human proclivity to love can overcome even the most devoted nihilist.

Without calling herself by the title, Anna is actually the most consistent nihilist. In spite of her own feelings, she never returns Bazarov's expression of love, and she sees only emptiness and pointlessness: "So many memories, and nothing to remember, and before me, before me—a long, long road, and no goal. . . . I have no wish to go on."[38] She *feels* the nothingness, the equally meaningless past and future. Anna's nihilism is not learned philosophically; it is something that she herself comes upon: "Sometimes coming out of her fragrant bath all warm and enervated, she would fall to musing on the nothingness of life, the sorrow, the labour, the malice of it. . . . Like all women who have not succeeded in loving, she wanted something, without herself knowing what. Strictly speaking, she wanted nothing; but it seemed to her that she wanted everything."[39] In most ways, but not in romance or friendship, she has the best of what the world has to offer; yet she remains profoundly unfulfilled.

Divergent dispositions to friendship and love eventually separate the characters, not only Anna from Bazarov, but also Bazarov and Arkady. True to his convictions, Bazarov denies the reality of friendship, repeatedly referring to Arkady as a fool, as the lesser sort of man who will need the domestication of marriage.

Nihilism is a grand negation; it negates friendship and love even with fellow nihilists. But as Arkady readily discovers, and Bazarov unwillingly does, friendship and romantic love are resistant to negation by an idea. In all forms of human love, the novelty and goodness of creation reemerge; such human love partakes of a spiritual force that cannot be permanently suppressed, not even by the most twisted philosophy.

The Question of Death

When Bazarov is stricken with typhus and is on his deathbed, a decent but apparently ineffective priest is drawn into the story (not unlike the narrative of *Manfred*). As last rites are administered, "when the holy oil touched his breast, one eye opened, and it seemed as though . . . something like a shudder of horror passed over the death-stricken face."[40] The dying nihilist is horrified at the touch of the sacraments, but because he can no longer speak, we might reasonably assume that he is dying with the same contempt for God with which he has lived. But with only one of his eyes left open to this world, perhaps he is horrified with himself. We cannot be completely sure.

If death is the last word, then its colorless formlessness contextualizes all other words and deeds. For those who die without hope, death arrives as the unqualified *nihil*, the annihilation of the living consciousness. But if death is not the final word, if it is both ending and opening, then it very differently colors all that precedes—and all that may follow.

In nineteenth-century nihilism, several centuries of criticism reach an end point. Given nihilism's negation of every value, "truth" requires scare quotes; it is merely an unreal abstraction that means nothing. In Bazarov's constricted worldview, what matters, and it does not matter all that much, is dissecting frogs.[‡] Nihilism is a corrosive and weakening philosophy that requires a perverse strength to be maintained. It can fit with resignation to the world as it is; and because it is easily alloyed, it can fit with murderous revolutionary activity to change the world.[41]

Revolutionary Morality: Deracinated, Hidden, and Distorted

In Christian understanding, God's transcendence is joined to immanence—in the goodness of creation and, in the most concentrated way, in the incarnation of the Son, the personal unification of transcendence and immanence. Christian faith is primarily relational; it is centered in each human person's relation to the incarnate Son and in each person's relation to all other persons. From this relational perspective, morality is a result, an important but always secondary reality. In relationship to the Son, and being made in the image and likeness of God, human persons cannot help but be concerned with morality. In individuals, communities, and historical periods, there is frequent thoughtlessness, moral failure, and gross evil; but the concern with morality never entirely disappears. The perpetual concern with morality indicates its derivation from a higher order. Being made in the image of a perfect, eternal, transcendent being does not allow us to sink to purely animalistic levels without discomfort.

‡ In a masterly stroke, Turgenev several times uses dissection to point to Bazarov's fundamental view of things. Bazarov's extreme empiricism leads him to deny that there is "science" or "medicine" or any general principles or universals. In his extreme reductionism, there are only ways to work upon nature, like dissection. When Bazarov says that he would like to see Anna's body on a dissecting table (p. 91), he is reducing sexual attraction to its component parts. But in Turgenev's coup de grâce, Bazarov gets infected with typhus from a small finger cut while dissecting a corpse (which he calls "it"), a man who had just died from the disease (p. 224).

Nonetheless, from the 1600s to the revolutionary stirrings of the mid-1800s, more and more intellectual leaders lost interest in Christian anthropology and morality, as they instead embraced mechanistic conceptions of nature, society, and individual. In this increasingly barren spiritual terrain, for people who ceased believing in God, the moral sense previously guided by faith became deracinated and homeless. No longer housed in a transcendent context, morality could be rededicated to purely immanental concerns—but not without fundamental distortions. From the French Revolution to modern totalitarianisms, progress was sought apart from God; but the deracinated and distorted moral sense instead plummeted humankind into what Diane Yeager called "the twentieth century's unprecedented lake of blood."[42] Second to none in murder, especially of their own people, were the followers of Frederick Engels and Karl Marx.[43]

Political Darkenings

Under the influence of Feuerbach, Marx and Engels turned from the God they no longer believed in to their revolutionary, atheistic vision for this world alone. Summarizing what he and Marx had learned from Feuerbach, Engels declared, "Nothing exists outside nature and man, and the higher beings our religious fantasies have created are only the fantastic reflection of our own essence."[44] Believing themselves liberated from a nonexistent God, Marx and Engels turned their moral energy to refashion human society; and they successfully persuaded millions to follow them in the revolutionary effort. Marx was highly pleased by what he took as Feuerbach's accomplishment, but he wanted to go beyond Feuerbach. Marx thus declared, "The philosophers have *interpreted* the world in various ways; the point however is to *change* it."[45] And change it Marx and Engels unquestionably did. From Russia to China to Cuba and myriad parts between, their followers have seized totalitarian power; and on every continent, they have never ceased infiltrating educational institutions. Even after the dissolution of the Soviet Union in 1989, many professors in universities around the world openly, clandestinely, or ignorantly support various forms of Marxism.

For many decades before the Russian Revolution of 1917, Europe, and especially Russia, witnessed a complicated mix of Marxism, nihilism, and anarchism, while various revolutionary strategies were conceived and activities initiated. Within this smoldering milieu, Sergei Nechaev infamously distinguished himself for dedication, and for duplicity—even to other revolutionaries. Nechaev's "The Catechism of the Revolutionary" was scorned by Marx, but Lenin declared it to be necessary reading for revolutionaries. Nechaev's "Catechism" was intended as yet another moral and religious replacement of Christianity.[46] His anarchic efforts knew no bounds. With cold depravity he even arranged the assassination of one of his own inner members, apparently to enforce group discipline.

Mikhail Bakunin was a Russian nobleman who promulgated collectivist anarchism. He was at first supportive of the younger Nechaev but eventually was put off by his mendacious duplicity. While devoted to revolution, Bakunin adamantly opposed Marx's notion of the dictatorship of the proletariat as a temporary state, because Bakunin foresaw that the dictatorship would not be temporary. Bakunin was first and foremost an advocate of freedom. He thus wished to eliminate the state and replace it with self-governing communes and workplaces, and he wished to eliminate God because he thought God's existence would limit human freedom. Hailing Satan as his heroic proto-revolutionary, Mikhail Bakunin wrote, "If God is, man is a slave; now, man can and must be free; then, God does not exist. . . . it will be necessary to eliminate, first of all, this fiction of God, the eternal absolute enslaver."[47] His belligerent atheism was typical of Europe's simmering insurgencies.

Also in the revolutionary, atheistic mélange was a group devoted to violent overthrow and assassination that called itself "Hell." The tactics of another revolutionary group, "People's Will," would be lauded and emulated by Lenin, whose elder brother was one of the movement's martyrs.[48] Consisting of only about thirty members, People's Will made seven assassination attempts on the tsar's life, the last of which succeeded. They wanted Alexander II dead because his policies, like liberating the serfs, were stabilizing the country; they were too good and thereby were preventing revolution.

Lenin, who was at the front of the 1917 Bolshevik Revolution and became the first communist ruler of Russia, was immersed in the literature of Russian nihilism. Strongly influenced by Chernyshevsky's nihilist novel *What Is to Be Done?*, Lenin wrote a book of the same title.[49] Lenin's book is a sustained polemic against ineffective organizers and all those merely aiming at reform, instead of the total overthrow of the ancien régime. His writing is imbued with revolutionary hardness, revealing a man frighteningly sure of himself and his public endeavors. The text displays the utter absence of grace and charity, as he exhorts readers toward the communist revolution that would enshroud a great nation, empire, and, later, much of the world.

Once the Russian Marxists seized power in 1917, it is no accident that militant atheism became official policy. Soviet communism saw itself in a life-or-death struggle with all other accounts of the meaning of human life and death. In this struggle, atheism was necessarily required—and required to be enforced. Thus Joseph Stalin's first five-year economic plan was accompanied by a "godless five-year plan." Reminiscent of the French Revolution's turning the Cathedral of Notre Dame into the Temple of Reason, but even worse, in Moscow in 1931 the magnificent Cathedral of Christ the Savior was destroyed, its deconstructed parts diverted to other building projects. In 1939, 8,000 churches were destroyed and 35,000 religious devotees were arrested. Much of the Orthodox Church's hierarchy was either exiled or murdered. In 1917, there had been about 50,000 churches in Russia; in 1939, there were less than 100.[50]

The all-encompassing attempt to govern human meaning did not stop at Christian faith; it targeted any compassion or morality other than the good of the Party. While Judaism, Christianity, and Kantian ethics prohibit lying, Party ethics demanded it whenever necessary for the Party's purposes. Against any lingering sense of compassion, communists were to overcome their hesitation to denounce, torture, or kill a class enemy. In official documents "conscience" was replaced with "class feeling." Lev Kopelev, at first an advocate of the Party and then one of its famous dissidents, reveals the depth of spiritual perversity: "Our great goal was the universal triumph of Communism, and for the sake of that goal everything was permissible—to lie, to steal, to destroy hundreds of thousands and even millions of people. . . . And to hesitate or doubt about all this was to give in to 'intellectual squeamishness' and 'stupid liberalism.'"[51] The Terror of the French Revolution had killed tens of thousands; the more enduring terror of the Russian Revolution would kill millions—and leave millions more morally stunted and paralyzed. The failure of the French Revolution should have been a warning rather than a prototype.

Looking at Marxism's global history of revolutions, wars, suppression of human freedom, economic failure, and architectural ugliness, and considering its repeated stifling of human happiness, it seems surprising that its variants keep cropping up. That such a path has so often been chosen suggests some kind of moral attraction. But the harm inevitably done also suggests that the attraction is linked to a critical underlying problem—a complicated phenomenon that Michael Polanyi (1891–1976) called *moral inversion*.

Marxism's Moral Inversion: Contradictory Couplings

Pondering how Marxists could openly deny normal moral standards and yet be seen by so many as champions against injustice, Polanyi asked,

> Why should so contradictory a doctrine carry such supreme convincing power? The answer is, I believe, that it enables the modern mind, tortured by moral self-doubt, to indulge its moral passions in terms which also satisfy its passion for ruthless objectivity.[52]

The increasing number of those who no longer believed in transcendent qualities like truth, goodness, and beauty—whose reductionist, scientific worldview was insistently mechanistic, naturalistic, and objectivist—were highly vulnerable to Marxism's offerings. The Marxist claim of objectivity appealed to their reductionist worldview at the same time that it housed and masked their moral passions. As

Polanyi put it, "The public, taught by the sociologist to distrust its traditional morality, is grateful to receive it back from him in a scientifically branded wrapping."[53] Even human beings thoroughly misguided in their thinking do not succeed in completely eliminating moral aspirations. For a growing number who considered God and morality to be fictions, the moral sense first became subterranean and then was easily diverted to serve other purposes—like the "scientific" attempt to construct a perfect society. But the suppressed moral sense, in someone who does not believe that there is such a thing and does not believe that he has one, becomes particularly dangerous.

Moral inversion always involves contradictory couplings, like joining the belief that there is no universal overarching truth to the belief that there could be unlimited social improvement. Elucidating Polanyi's complex notion, Yeager characterized moral inversion as

> the process by which the fusion of scientific skepticism . . . with utopian social aspirations . . . produces the dystopia of moral and political nihilism out of which arises the modern totalitarian state, in which the only principle of social order is absolute coercive power and in which material welfare is embraced as the supreme social good.[54]

By the time Marx's writings became an international ferment, the withering effects of mechanistic, naturalistic views had for over two centuries been draining the European soul, rendering it ripe for a catastrophic harvest. In Polanyi's terms, "The morally inverted person has not merely performed a philosophic substitution of moral aims by material purposes, but is acting with the whole force of his homeless moral passions within a purely materialistic framework of purposes."[55] The twisted genius of Marxism, and the secret of its attractiveness, was its combination of scientific skepticism with a hidden, displaced, and misdirected moral sense.

To succeed, Marx had to turn European nihilists from extreme individualism (much like the fictitious Bazarov) to his communist vision for the whole of humanity. The communist vision had the advantage of promising power and "scientific" inevitability—surreptitiously arousing the moral sense which nihilists did not believe they had. Polanyi contended that "the conversion of the nihilist from extreme individualism to the service of a fierce and narrow political creed is the turning-point of the European Revolution."[56] This Marxist revolution has been compared to a second Enlightenment,[57] even more anti-religious than the first and even more skeptical. While the first and the second shared the quest for universality, the first did so, especially in Kant, with respect for individual freedom; the second, claiming to be on the right side of the inevitable materialist march of history, would prove itself the unparalleled nemesis of individual freedom.

Looking to science as the archetype of all authentic knowledge, Marx offered both nihilists and idealists a vision for the future of humankind, where the injustices of the old order would pass away and a new, scientifically ordered humanity would come to pass. What Marx offered was almost a parody of the biblical, Pauline promise: "So if anyone is in Christ, there is a new creation: everything old has passed away; [behold], everything has become new!" (2 Cor 5:17). Polanyi observed about Marx's proposal, "Though this prospect was put forward as a purely scientific observation, it endowed those who accepted it with a feeling of overwhelming moral superiority."[58] To any follower of Christ, the attractiveness of this inverted morality can only seem strange; however, in the spiritually scorched landscape of mid-nineteenth- and early twentieth-century Europe, where Christ seemed to many a distant legend of a superstitious era, the Marxist option could appear seductively meaningful.

Generally speaking, the modern West has not suffered from a lack of moral passion, but from its excess.[59] As Polanyi colorfully asked, "What sluggish river has ever broken the dams which contained it, or smashed the wheels which harnessed it?"[60] Historically, classical morality was, among other virtues, a question of temperance, serenity, composure, and restraint. But from the opening days of the French Revolution, moral passion was joined to a driving sense of moral impatience, whose guiding principle was the unlimited improvement of individuals and their society. Previously in the Christian-dominated West, human society was sculpted between interaction with the laws of nature and foundational beliefs in a higher, transcendent purpose. The promise of life after death, the hope of heaven, has a moderating effect on human passion, moral and otherwise. But if the promise is demoted to a fiction of naïve superstition, the human desire for perfection—which emphatically remains—tends to be redirected from the patient expectation of eternity to unbridled passion for immediate and comprehensive improvements in the political realm and its citizenry. This first step is already perilous; but when it is enacted by those who have become skeptical about the existence of God and morality based upon relation to God, moral inversion occurs and careens toward destructive events like the Russian Revolution and its murderous aftermath. Stricken by moral inversion, a society retains the latent force of Christian morality but has lost its tempering influence.

Christianity offers a unified vision of nature, culture, and Spirit in which culture is a vital but always intermediary realm between nature, with which we must interact, and God, with whom we must choose to interact. While Christians may care greatly about culture, such cares are tempered by believing that there is something greater than culture—and that we will be part of this greater, future, and forever reality. But once belief in God is no longer operative, once humanity and its culture are seen as the highest reality, the grounds of humility are gone. In the past, Christians have actively opposed social or political wrongs like slavery, but the opposition was the result of Christian faith, not its center. Moreover, Jesus called for the humility to recognize our own shortcomings (sin), to take the log out of our own eye before trying to remove the speck from another's (Matt 7:5). Politics is always an imperfect art exercised by imperfect people. But without the tempering effects of faith and the spiritual grounding of humility, there is likely to be impatience, anger, and ferocity at any resistance to implementing the morally inverted, exclusively immanental vision.

The Promethean attempt to infuse ultimate meaning into secular affairs has demanded unquestioning loyalty to the revolutionary cause, as it labors to transpose a formerly deferred heavenly glory to here-and-now interactions right before the eyes. In such attempts all ethical thought and action must be subjected to an imperious immediacy. As Polanyi observed, "To achieve a comprehensive improvement of society you need comprehensive powers; so you must regard all resistance to yourself as high treason and must put it down mercilessly."[61] Willingness to crush human opponents is propelled by the displaced and distorted morality hidden in the revolutionary propensity: justice must be achieved without delay. Yet from Nechaev's slaughtering of *one* member of his revolutionary cell to Stalin's slaughtering of tens of millions, we can only shudder at the inhuman implementation of these inverted principles.

Believing that there is no overarching truth, and hence no overarching morality, creates a vacuum for the ominous invention and imposition of what counts as meaningful. For Marxist rulers, the world of constant material changes needed the Party to provide stability by overseeing the changes. As Yeager observed, this kind of power takes on a life of its own: "The energy and commitment become immune to public criticism, to self-conscious review, and, perhaps most importantly, to any form of restraint."[62] For Marxists in power, reality was no longer a given, but something negotiable, to be constructed rather than discovered. The Party would determine what is factual and what is not. Hence, because the Party determines objectivity, in the service of the Party, lies were not lies. Thus in *1984*, George Orwell rightly observed that in totalitarian regimes, merely believing in reality is subversive, for reality is the objective component of truth.[63] Denying something so basic as reality and its irremovable place in the discovery of truth makes totalitarianism inherently unstable; truth will out. While its rule lasts, Marxism's internal contradictions can only be sustained through coercion and violence.

There is a strange relationship between unlimited individualism and state totalitarianism: both miss the centrality of persons in relations. Romanticism, when it descends to a nihilism of the individual, places no moral or social limit on those bold enough to break through all limits. Marxism (and fascism), a nihilism of the collectivity, places no limit on the power of the governing state. Perhaps the worst aspect of Marxism's moral inversion is that it coercively subordinates thought, speech, and social interaction to its central governing power, imposing repugnant encroachments on human intellect, freedom, and dignity.

From the French Revolution to the Russian, the allure of naturalizing the supernatural has proved deadly. Attempting to capture the energy of a formerly believed-in God and pour it into strictly human affairs is doomed from the outset.

Concluding Reflections: "Inhuman Humanism"

Since the Enlightenment, the West has been in the business of inventing exclusive humanisms. Usually undertaken on behalf of humankind, such exclusive humanism has invariably become what Henri de Lubac called "inhuman humanism."[64] Having gone through Reformation, Enlightenment, and French Revolution, the West then veered from Romanticism to nihilism to new forms of revolutionary totalitarianism. Secular alternatives to Christian faith have brought millions down a path steeply sloping toward catastrophe. As the Hebrew proverb warned, "There is a way that seems right . . . but its end is the way to death" (Prov 14:12).

How the transcendent God became for so many an antagonist to be overcome is a long, multifaceted, and difficult story to tell. But in many ways it is our story. In Dostoevsky's view, the cause of the descent was clear: "Repudiate Christ and the human mind can arrive at the most astonishing conclusions."[65] In repudiating Christ, Russian Marxism sank to astonishing levels of soul-suppression and mass murder. Nonetheless, what is most remarkable is that so many Russians withstood the persecutions. A 1937 survey showed that 56 percent of the Russian people still believed in God. In the infamous labor camps, where torture and lonely death were ever-present possibilities, Christian believers often distinguished themselves by their fortitude. Numerous memoirs record that, when put to the most severe tests, *only* the religious believers chose to follow their conscience over avoidance of suffering and execution.[66]

The mirage of the immanental utopia has not disappeared. Those who cease believing in God do not cease believing. From the Russian

Revolution to current iterations in China, North Korea, Cuba, and elsewhere, there have been attempts to control the beliefs of every individual and the collective whole. Because, according to an old Russian proverb, "a sacred space is never empty,"[67] the relative health or sickness of an era will be determined by what beliefs and practices occupy the sacred space.

The dissolution of the belief that we are sons and daughters of God, citizens of creation, has exacted a great cost. To cease interest in the "fruit of the Spirit"—"love, joy, peace, patience, kindness, generosity, faithfulness, gentleness, and self-control" (Gal 5:22-23)—and to replace these transcendent qualities with exclusively human endeavors and outlooks—unlimited self-expression, nihilism, anarchism, or Marxism—predictably led to personal and social disaster. As David Bentley Hart put it, "The consequences of so great a joy rejected are a sorrow, bewilderment, and anxiety for which there is no precedent."[68] And we might add, for which there is no necessity.

3
ENDEAVORS IN DARKNESS I
Auguste Comte and Positivism

> Herr Feuerbach in Berlin, like Monsieur Comte in Paris, offers Christian Europe a new god to worship—the human race.
> **Emile Saisset**

> The positive philosophy, with all its natural superiority, will be able to displace entirely the theological and metaphysical philosophies.
> **Auguste Comte**

> Comte remains one of the secret rulers of our world, pointing the way to human self-deification and an evisceration of authentic political life.
> **Daniel J. Mahoney**

> A great many people today are unknowingly positivists in that they claim to believe only statements supported by tangible evidence.
> **Mary Pickering**[1]

Born into the intellectual, social, and religious chaos of postrevolutionary France, Auguste Comte (1798–1857) proposed a systematic plan for achieving a new basis of order and progress, first in Europe and then throughout the world. Calling his plan *positivism*, Comte greatly expanded upon principles of Francis Bacon (1561–1626). Comte held that every competent thinker agrees "that there can be no real knowledge except that which rests upon observed facts."[2] Focusing solely on factual observation, Comte sought to limit human knowledge to five categories, "astronomical, physical, chemical, physiological, and social phenomena," and thereby render "all our fundamental conceptions . . . homogeneous."[3] From this base, what we might call the hard sciences—along with the significant addition of social phenomena—Comte wanted positivism to become not just a consensus, but a creed: a universal philosophy that would guide humankind along the pathway of unlimited progress.

Focusing only on realities whose truth can be demonstrated, Comte coupled factual observation with an ironclad prohibition on anything alleged to be transcendent. While Comte's denial of transcendence and dismissal of Christianity were not by his time unusual, he went further in attempting to replace Christianity with his own exclusively humanist religion. His destructive intent for Christianity was clear and extreme: "*To destroy, you must replace.*"[4] As we shall see, Comte's replacement religion has not developed as he envisioned; but unnamed, it has had an ongoing, indirect kind of success that continues to compete with Christianity. In Daniel J. Mahoney's assessment, "In multiple ways, Auguste Comte remains the secret ruler of souls."[5] Although they are not often recognized as Comte's, many of his ideas have become common presuppositions, broadly inculcated in contemporary universities.

Comte's nineteenth century was a time when multiple options arose for understanding human meaning, identity, and purpose. In our own time, many of these fundamental options, what Brad Gregory calls "Life Questions,"[6] have become mixed and muddled; and many contemporary people hold views or are affected by views whose historical precedents are mostly hidden from sight—views like Comte's. Uncovering the thought of this gifted and dangerous foe of faith will further our efforts to understand the historical roots of contemporary challenges to faith.

Auguste Comte's Positivist Vision

During Comte's lifetime there were nine different governments and revolutions, as France's politics veered between mob rule and dictatorship and its religious life continued to fragment. Trying to overcome this anarchic situation, Comte proposed a systematic, all-encompassing vision—a new social, intellectual, and spiritual order.

Gifted in mathematics, Comte was admitted in 1814 to the prestigious École Polytechnique, where he began to conceive the role science could play in social reconstruction. However, in 1816, having already ceased believing in God, he was expelled for leading a student revolt.[7]

The disjunction between Comte's private and public life was stark. He sought to establish a public harmony that was almost totally lacking in his private life, which was strewn with severe psychological difficulties, broken relationships, and delusions of religious grandeur.[8]

After his expulsion from the École Polytechnique, Comte became the secretary of Henri de Saint-Simon, who was himself attempting a utopian social reconstruction. But in Comte's recurrent pattern of ruined relationships, he broke off his attachment to Saint-Simon in great bitterness and never thereafter acknowledged Saint-Simon's influence.[9] Likewise, Comte's marriage painfully failed. Yet believing marriage to be indissoluble, Comte financially supported his ex-spouse all his life. Similarly, his main French follower Émile Littré as well as John Stuart Mill eventually broke off their relationships with Comte. At least some of his relational difficulties should be attributed to a documented psychological disorder. In 1826 Comte offered a course on positivism attended by many great scientists. But after the third lecture, he went mad and spent eight months in an asylum for manic depression.[10] Although the treatment was apparently not successful, Comte commendably remained productive by establishing his own highly disciplined regimen.

Positivism: An All-Encompassing Project

Comte saw that the French Revolution had shattered the old order; he characterized his time as "a century in which a general reconstruction is everywhere the chief want."[11] He repeatedly expressed concern about the anarchy of his time, whose origins he attributed to "the irremediable weakness of the old beliefs."[12] Not lacking in confidence, Comte believed that his methods, his teachings about nature and society, and his religion would rectify the chaos and provide the order for a new world foundation, the base from which humanity could progress. He envisioned that "the revolution of Western Europe will proceed in a free and systematic course towards its peaceful termination, under the direction of the true servants of Humanity."[13] These "true servants of Humanity" would be those who adopted and implemented his system of positivism.

Comte thought that Western Europe would no longer submit to unprovable and completely illusory Christian views: "For such is the character of all opinions of theological origin, whatever the theology be, be it even the purest Deism."[14] Believing that Christianity and even the Deism of the Enlightenment were nothing more than deep-seated illusions, Comte did not attempt a point-by-point critique, because he considered such critical engagements to be confined within the *negative*, against which the very title of *positivism* was intended. Instead of critique, he launched positivism as a new foundation for humanity, a way of understanding material things, biological life, humanity, and religion. Comte made the aphorism "*To destroy, you must replace*" a guiding tenet: "This principle is adopted and systematically developed by Positivism."[15] From the earliest days of Christianity, believers have often successfully engaged atheists (and people of other faiths). However, it is exceedingly difficult, if not futile, to engage someone whose goal is first to annihilate your faith and then to replace it, so that it will never rise again. From a Christian perspective, Comte's project is far worse than atheism.

Comte asked his contemporaries to cease thinking of themselves as related to a nonexisting God, and he was convinced that positivism's demonstrable results would facilitate people to give up the God-fantasy: "These chimerical hopes, these exaggerated ideas of man's importance in the universe, to which the theological philosophy gives rise, are destroyed irrevocably by the first fruits of the positive philosophy."[16] To accomplish his grandiose vision of reestablishing order and directing humanity toward unending progress, Comte declared that positivism would have to take the reins from Christianity: "In the name of the Past and of the Future, the servants of Humanity—both its philosophical and practical servants—come forward to claim as their due the general direction of this world. . . . they exclude, once for all, from political supremacy, all the different servants of God—Catholic, Protestant, or Deist—as being at once behindhand

and a cause of disturbance."[17] Christians, whom Comte saw as servants of an imaginary Deity, were guilty of obstructing progress and needed to be ousted from positions of political and cultural influence. In their stead the positivist movement would take on what rightly belonged to them—"the general direction of this world." Such claims were not uncommon in the nineteenth century; Marx and his communist followers made similar claims, as did Charles Fourier and his socialist followers. After the eruption of the French Revolution and its calamitous collapse, intellectual leaders sensed that the momentum of centuries had been halted. The world really did seem as though it were up for grabs.

Comte's effort to regenerate humanity proceeded by an interlocking progression of the sciences. Mathematics allowed the development of astronomy; physics permitted the development of chemistry, which then led to the development of biology. But the final science that was needed to coordinate all the others, Comte's grand culmination, was the science of society. This final and culminating science Comte called either "social physics" or "sociology"—a term he originated.[18] Comte thought social physics the most pressing science of his time. Since great progress had already been made in astronomical, physical, chemical, and physiological knowledge, it only remained to focus on social physics: "I aim at impressing upon this last branch of our knowledge the same positive character that already marks all the other branches. If this condition is once really fulfilled, the philosophical system of the modern world will be founded at last in its entirety; for there is no observable fact that would not then be included in one or another of the five great categories."[19] Comte knew that there would be much ongoing work in each field to be done; however, all foundational conceptions would then be "homogeneous," philosophy would be on its firm and unchangeable foundation, and indefinite progress would be possible with further observation and development of theory.

A central principle of Comte's positivism was its sweeping claim about humanity's historical development. He claimed that he had "discovered a great fundamental law, to which the mind is subjected by an invariable necessity." In this discovery, "each of our principle conceptions, each branch of our knowledge, passes in succession through three different theoretical states: the theological or fictitious state, the metaphysical or abstract state, and the scientific or positive state."[20] In Comte's historical scheme, the first theological stage is a necessary starting point, the second metaphysical stage is transitional, and the third stage is "fixed and definitive"—the human mind supposedly having arrived at its mature foundation.[21]

The historically less mature, theological state is concerned with first and final causes of phenomena. But where first and final causes try to answer *why*, Comte's methodological principle insistently limited itself to asking *how things work*. Christian theology (and even Deism) attributes the ultimate first cause to be the Creator God. The final cause, especially in Catholic theology, is God himself, who attracts all things in creation to seek their highest good.[22] But according to Comte, the concern with first and final causes is a manifestation of humanity's less mature stage. Nonetheless, Comte believed that this first theological stage is both inevitable and necessary for human development, and, with few exceptions, universal. Without engaging any particulars of Christian thought (or any other world religion), Comte's comprehensive, historical classification effectively relegated Christianity to a fossil-like status.

The second, metaphysical stage was merely transitional, replacing theological, supernatural agents with abstract forces.[23] Comte had no love for this transitional, metaphysical Deism of the Enlightenment, seeing its critical stance as the opposite of positivism—a negative enterprise partially responsible for the chaos of the Revolution and its aftereffects.

The third and final stage was positivism, which ceases all interest in origins (first causes) and final causes. Instead, the positive state, "by reasoning and observation," is concerned with laws of phenomena, "their invariable relations of succession and likeness."[24] Positivism can be concerned with particular phenomena or "general facts," i.e., theories about those facts.[25] However, the focus of positivism is on this world alone. Even the most complete positivist explanations "do not pretend to explain the real causes of phenomena."[26] Instead, Comte sought to restrict human endeavor to asking *how* rather than *why*, believing that the restriction would lead to inevitable progress by focusing on the real, i.e., the positive.

Believing questions of first and final causes to be insoluble, Comte eliminates them in favor of the positive reality that is always before our eyes. Comte thus held that theology—thinking about God—and positivist thinking are "profoundly incompatible."[27] In Comte's view, monotheism, the peak of theological development, and Catholicism, the peak of Christianity, have had their day, have already played out their historical roles. But now "the positive philosophy, with all its natural superiority, will be able to displace entirely the theological and metaphysical philosophies."[28] Having already decided that theology and Christian faith have nothing real to offer, Comte saw his positive philosophy as the continuation, systemization, and development of the trend begun by Bacon, Descartes, and Galileo.[29] Comte's insistence that all thinking be directed only to verifiable facts picks up the historical thread from Bacon to David Hume and makes it foundational. At its roots, positivism was defined as focusing on what was real, useful, certain, and precise. Instead of seeking absolute knowledge, as in theology or metaphysics, knowledge should be pursued relative to human need, i.e., for constructive social purposes.[30] Positivism first limits human attention to this world alone and then mounts a constructive program of how to think and act in this world.

It is tempting to classify Comte's positivism as reductionistic scientism, and indeed Comte did argue that real knowledge only comes through "observation, experimentation, and comparison."[31] Moreover, Comte would have us vastly reduce the scope of human aims: "Our intellectual activity is sufficiently excited by the mere hope of discovering the laws of phenomena, by the simple desire of verifying or disproving a theory."[32] But unlike reductionism, where the lower level is believed to be the most real, Comte reverses direction, believing each ascending level, from physics to chemistry to biology to human life, to be more complex and more real than the one that preceded it—with sociology being the most real and the most complex.

Comte unquestionably reduces everything real to this world alone; however, having limited everything to this world, he puts forward levels of ascending rank that cannot be reduced to the lower rank(s). Moreover, in a move that some of his most illustrious followers found ridiculous, Comte attempted to infuse positivism with religious fervor by inventing whole cloth a new Religion of Humanity.

The Religion of Humanity

For positivism to succeed as a way of life, Comte knew that he needed "a central point round which all will naturally meet."[33] Without such a center he feared that positivism could not successfully replace the synthesis that Christian thought and practice had once achieved. Convinced that human society was the highest reality that was unquestionably real, Comte settled on worshiping humanity: "All our thoughts, feelings, and actions flow spontaneously to a common centre in Humanity, our Supreme Being; a Being who is real, accessible, and sympathetic, because she is of the same nature as her worshippers, though far superior to any one of them."[34] While transferring worship from a (nonexistent) God to a clearly existing humanity, all the attributes formerly attributed to God could not be transferred: "The Great Being whom we worship is not immutable any more than it is absolute. Its nature is relative; and, as such, eminently capable of growth. . . . the most vital of all living beings known to us."[35] However, the relative, changing nature of the Great Being means that each one can contribute to its *progress*—the idée fixe of positivism. The growth of humanity occurs over generations as human beings progress individually and thus contribute to the Great Being. Human beings are both participants in and producers of our own Deity: "Every great or good man will feel that his own life is an indispensable element in the great organism. The supremacy of Humanity is but the result of individual cooperation; her power is not supreme, it is only superior to that of all beings whom we know."[36] Asking people to contribute to something greater than themselves was at least psychologically appealing. There is something in Comte's teachings that always seems to live next door to the truth.

Holding humanity to be the Supreme Being—the ultimate object of worship—is an unusual twist of atheism. Yet Comte's worship of humanity was completely earnest and, in its way, even a simulacrum of piety: "Towards Humanity, who is for us the only truly Great Being, we, the conscious elements of whom she is composed, shall henceforth direct every aspect of our life, individual or collective. Our thoughts will be devoted to the knowledge of Humanity, our affections to her love, our actions to her service."[37] Comte's call to love and service can be seen as an uprooting and tampering with Jesus' second love command: "Love your neighbor as yourself" (Mark 12:31). Having discarded the greater context of Jesus' first love command, to love *God* with heart, soul, mind, and strength, Comte tried to co-opt and redirect what remained—the love of humanity.

Comte's motto for the Religion of Humanity was not without merit: "Love, then, is our principle; Order our basis; and Progress our end."[38] In fact, he thought the whole system of positivism rests upon the principle of love: "It is the peculiar characteristic of the Great Being."[39] Exhorting the love of others, about 1850 he coined the term "altruism."[40] He held that an outward, altruistic orientation was essential to the health of the individual soul: "The individual must subordinate himself to an existence outside itself in order to find in it the source of his own stability. And this condition cannot be effectually realized except under the impulse of propensities prompting him to live for others."[41] Here again Comte's atheistic echo of Jesus' love commands is a neighbor to the truth, a human attempt to generate living water.

True Believers

For large segments, but by no means all, of the nineteenth-century West, Christianity had ceased to be an authoritative approach to truth. For some it just needed to prune "myths" like incarnation and resurrection; for others, it was something to be mocked; but for Comtians, it needed to be destroyed.

In contrast to the allegedly passé Christianity, we get a flavor of the excitement of Comte's alternative faith from Dr. Jean-François

Eugène Robinet, who had attended Comte's lectures: "In those hallowed hours that heralded such great destinies, we felt the breath of Humanity, we caught a glimpse of its reality, its greatness, we bowed before it and the holy enthusiasm of demonstrated faith was kindled for ever in our hearts."[42] The enthusiasm was joined to the universality at which Comte aimed: "The union of Western Europe is but a preliminary step to the union of Humanity."[43] Comte could not resist crowing over his allegedly superior alternative: "The whole effect of positivist worship will be to make men feel clearly how far superior in every respect is the synthesis founded on the love of Humanity to that founded on the love of God."[44] With similar exuberance, another disciple polemically declared,

> We have faith which inspires great things and the courage which spurs us on to achieve them. Against the fragrance of your incense and the harmony of your canticles we set up the splendid festivals of Humanity in the holy city of the Revolution: against the cult of God we set the cult of woman and of the great men who have made us what we are: against the narrow mysticism of the Catholic, the noble activity of the citizen and the enthusiasm of the Republicans of '92. We shall convince the men, we shall persuade the women, and the day is not far off when we shall enter your forsaken temples as masters, bearing above our heads the banner of triumphant Humanity.[45]

Comte and his followers were true believers, confident that Christianity would be replaced by the Religion of Humanity. Calling himself the Great Priest of Humanity, in 1851 Comte boldly predicted his installation at Notre Dame: "I am convinced that before the year 1860 I shall be preaching positivism at Notre Dame as the only real and complete religion."[46] While Comte's prediction now seems like indulgence in fantasy, it should be remembered that in 1793, just a few years before Comte's birth, the Jacobins had in fact taken over Notre Dame and rededicated it as the Temple of Reason.

The French Revolution had tried and failed to enact a new anthropic vision. Comte likewise proposed a master plan for the human race.

His positivist religion thus imitated Catholicism's sacraments, with the new religion initiating nine sacraments instead of Catholicism's seven. Like the recent Revolution had done, Comte also created his own positivist calendar, with thirteen months, each with twenty-eight days, and each day and month named after a positivist hero. Moses, Confucius, Mohammed, and other religious names of note (e.g., St. Paul) were included; significantly, Jesus, whom Comte attacked as a "false founder" and "essentially a charlatan," was not.[47] Other luminaries like Homer, Aristotle, Charlemagne, William Shakespeare, Johannes Gutenberg, René Descartes, and Isaac Newton were included. Comte's attempt to create his own sacraments and then to rename and reorganize time are further indicators of the grandiose seriousness of his project.

While Comte apparently could not promise resurrection from the dead, he did create a celebration called the Day of All the Dead (cf. All Souls Day). On this day the worthiest souls were to be venerated in specially created sacred groves. Seven years after death, a soul was to be judged by the positivist priests, who would determine whether the deceased had been a servant of humanity. Only those deemed worthy would be buried in the civic cemeteries, and only the worthiest would be buried in the sacred groves, where they would be publicly commemorated. Criminals and antisocial types were to be buried and forgotten in unmarked graves.[48]

Important components of Comte's religion—love, altruism, and devotion to the social whole—are taken from or are similar to Christian teachings and are still widely affirmed, even among atheists. Nonetheless, his religion in its own right is virtually defunct. It was, in Thomas Huxley's jibe, merely "Catholicism minus Christianity."[49]

Comte's hope that the *formal*, positivist worship of humanity would prevail over the worship of God has not been realized; however, in one or another of its protean forms, quasi-religious devotion to exclusivist humanism has continued apace. There is a recurrent illusion that next time, if only done rightly, Babel will be built; humanity will successfully engineer its own utopia. Comte's humanist vision was the epitome of this illusion.

The Significance of Comte

Comte's writings were a mixture of brilliance, insane fantasy, and an all-too-familiar attempt to expunge faith in God. His strategic choice not to attack Christianity directly should be understood as a meta-attack, meant not merely to wound but to annihilate. The intention was to render Christianity so irrelevant that no one in future would need to attack. Comte did not like being classified as an atheist, because he thought that atheism was not fully emancipated; stuck on the second historical stage of metaphysics, atheism can only perpetuate fruitless questions. More radically, Comte thought that atheism tries to answer a question that should no longer even be asked. Once positivism had presented its superior alternative, we were not only to cease believing in God, but also to cease arguing about God—and even to cease talking about God.

Comte's positivism combined scientific, utopian, and religious views. His religion began by assuming that there is no God who has created us and could help us; it ended with Comte declaring himself the High Priest of Humanity. Yet while his formal Religion of Humanity is a dust long ago dispersed, it was a prototype of things to come—of fashioning one's own religion or spirituality. However, Comte would not have approved of our current trend, in which individuals claim to be "spiritual but not religious," because he thought that society must have a well-defined common religion, not just individualistic attempts at spirituality. He thought that neither Protestantism, because of its individualistic tendencies, nor the critical philosophy of the Enlightenment would work: "While the Protestants and the deists have always attacked religion in the name of God, we must discard God, once and for all, in the name of religion."[50] Ever aiming at progress, Comte essentially contended that humankind had always, unwittingly, been worshiping itself.[51] Positivist religion made the worship of humanity explicit.

By choosing to worship humanity, Comte placed so much weight on the venerated social whole that he endangered the value and rights of the individual, a danger exacerbated by reiterated claims that individuals had duties, not rights. He made a bad matter worse in saying,

"The only real life is the collective life of the race; . . . individual life has no existence except as an abstraction."[52] Comte's abasement of individual life is profoundly anti-personal, a regressive antithesis of the eternal value with which Christianity views each human person. Moreover, in Christian thought, society can be valuable, even treasured, but it is never ultimate and certainly not worshiped. Instead, because a personal God transcends human society and the persons who constitute society, we may indeed owe all that we are to God—but not to our society. Hence, we are free to affirm or reject aspects of society—freedom that Comte's autocratic views did not countenance. In fact, John Stuart Mill, who had been one of Comte's most devoted followers, wrote that he was not sure whether he should weep or laugh at Comte's later, "decadent" attempt to invent a religion.[53] The disaffected Mill called Comte's religious writings about society (*Système de politique positive*) "the completest system of spiritual and temporal despotism which ever yet emanated from a human brain . . ."[54] Likewise, Henri de Lubac perceived a clear threat in Comte's teachings: "The positivist formula spells total tyranny."[55] Comte's autocratic views have not gained anything like the traction of his more empirical teachings.

Comte's positivism has enjoyed a wide success, but is not as well-known as the more recent logical positivists (sometimes called *neopositivists*) of the Vienna Circle.[56] Permeating social institutions beyond philosophy, the fundamental principles of positivism are now broadly assumed. As the eminent Comte scholar Mary Pickering observes, "A great many people today are unknowingly positivists in that they claim to believe only statements supported by tangible evidence."[57] By adopting this positivist emphasis on tangible, empirical evidence, people who know little or nothing about Comte, especially in the Western educational system, have perpetuated Comte's program.

In Western education, something like Comte's "social physics" has ascended to dominance, with the pervasiveness of such things as "outcomes assessment" and professional teacher training reduced to what is observable, comparable, and measurable.[58] By sending their children to parochial schools, or else homeschooling them, millions of parents today spend considerable amounts of money, time, or effort fleeing the effects of positivism.

In the political realm Comte's positivism also experienced some success, having been semiofficially adopted by the French Third Republic (1870–1940) for use in schools to combat Catholic influence. Positivism had an especially strong influence in Latin America and Brazil. Brazil's flag, for example, still displays Comte's motto of "Order and Progress." And there is still a lone positivist church in Rio de Janeiro.[59]

We can recognize Comte's genius and even his good intentions; his proposals were undoubtedly sincere. But from a Christian perspective, assessing Comte must begin and end with his dogmatically assumed starting point: the denial of transcendence. There is something pathetically predictable about a project that would advance humanity by denying the light of divine transcendence. Political philosopher Eric Voegelin did not look kindly upon Comte, seeing Comte's attempt to divinize society as one of the many failed instances of "immanentizing the meaning of existence."[60] Once Comte had ruled out the human relation to divine transcendence, the relation that makes human life so deeply meaningful, Comte was in no position to gauge the large lines of human history. Thus Voegelin considered Comte's law of three phases "a piece of fallacious speculation on the meaning of history which interpreted itself as the discovery of an empirical law."[61] Comte's so-called law is based on an unstated and unverifiable presupposition: the denial that anything or anyone transcends humanity. And yet, a century after Comte, every French undergraduate was still taught "the law of three states."[62] The positivist denial of transcendence has insinuated itself into the fabric of Western thought.

If we live in a divine creation, then the systematic rejection of transcendence cuts us off from what matters most, from the noblest human possibility—our relation to God. If we do not live in a divine creation, if humanity is a random development of an accidental universe, then Comte's proposals for love, social harmony, and progress have all the force of a personal preference. Altruism—the term he invented—really is central to his social project. However, by rejecting Jesus' first command to wholeheartedly love God, Comte deracinates Jesus' second command to love the neighbor (Mark 12:30-31). The second love command has always drawn its power and sustainability from the first. Once prescinded from the first, the second, unattached, devolves to personal preference. Millions of our contemporaries, including agnostics and atheists, commendably share Comte's preference for altruism, for love of others. Yet others—men like Pol Pot, Joseph Stalin, Mao Zedong, Adolf Hitler, and Benito Mussolini —will continue to have other preferences.

From a Christian perspective, Comte's call for love of others and concern for the social whole seems so sensible and innocent. It is at first difficult to see any objection. The profound problem, however, is not in the beneficent precipitate of Comte's thought; it is rather in the studied omission of what transcends, grounds, and actually does motivate love and service. Comte's ideas have a way of quietly occupying space previously accorded to Jesus' thought, crowding out the transcendent original with an utterly immanental counterfeit.

Comte wanted positivism to become the new global consensus; instead, in responding to the Life Questions, questions of the ultimate meaning and purpose of life, it has become one more option among many. Among religious believers differences are to one degree or another inevitable, but disagreements about whether God or humanity is the highest reality can only lead to a broad range of unreconcilable incompatibilities. Across the spectrum of contemporary culture, believers and unbelievers are now working to implement opposing principles. As a result, there is bound to be conflict and mutual incomprehension, accompanied by strident public discourse about education, politics, morality, and religion. The battle that Comte thought was over has only become more complicated.

4

ENDEAVORS IN DARKNESS II

Nietzsche's War on Christian Faith

I call Christianity the one great curse, the one great innermost corruption, the one great instinct of revenge, for which no means is poisonous, stealthy, subterranean, *small* enough—I call it the one immortal blemish of mankind.

Christianity was from the beginning, essentially and fundamentally, life's nausea and disgust with life, merely concealed behind, masked by, dressed up as, faith in "another" or "better" life.

The critic of Christianity cannot be spared the task of making Christianity look *contemptible*.

Friedrich Nietzsche

The epistemological skepticism and ontological nihilism implicit in [Nietzsche's] rigorous exercise of suspicion have become the unexamined conventional wisdom of the intellectual class that occupies the so-called humanities in countless college and university faculties.

Reinhard Hütter

Like the Marxist, though after another fashion and for other ends, the Nietzschean is a revolutionary.

The principal attack . . . is no longer an historical, metaphysical, political or social problem. It is a *spiritual* problem. It is the human problem as a whole. Today it is not one of the bases or one of the consequences of Christianity that is exposed to attack: the stroke is aimed directly at its heart.

Henri de Lubac[1]

Nietzsche's life (1844–1900) was marked with early grief, serious health issues, and, especially in his final years, unbearable loneliness. He had fond memories of his father, a kindly Lutheran pastor who died shortly before his fifth birthday. Nietzsche later wrote, "Although I was still very young and inexperienced, I did have some idea of death;

the thought of being separated forever from my beloved father seized me, and I wept bitterly."[2] About one year later grief struck again when Nietzsche's little brother Ludwig Joseph died suddenly. The night before the little child died, Nietzsche had a strange, prophetic dream. In the dream, while loud funereal organ music was playing, his deceased father came out of a grave, quickly entered the church, and taking a small child in his arms, returned to the tomb, the cover closing over both figures as the music ceased. Nietzsche later wrote, "Our grief was overwhelming."[3]

We can only guess at how these childhood calamities affected him. But we do know that self-identity was a lifelong issue for Nietzsche, because by his mid-twenties, he had already written nine autobiographical essays. Like Auguste Comte, he became an atheist at a young age.

By the mid-nineteenth century, atheism had become common; what is uncommon is the ferocity with which Nietzsche embraced atheism, his all-out war against Christianity. He did not see Christian faith as merely a mistaken outlook, but rather as a deadly poison that must be counteracted.

Major movements of human thought and culture have often been synthesized in an outstanding figure. In music, for example, Johann Sebastian Bach (1685–1750), born when the Baroque period was already well underway, creatively synthesizes Baroque trends and becomes its greatest exemplar. Similarly, the atheist movement is well underway when Nietzsche is born, but it comes to full fruition in him, with his open hostility toward faith in God, his attempted overthrow of morality and truth based on such faith, and the creative artistry with which he writes.

Nietzsche's writing is driven by his belief that Christianity is thoroughly false and, through centuries of criticism of the Bible and the church, had already been made unbelievable. Launching a direct attack on everything Christian, he articulates the most radical reversal of Judeo-Christian concepts of truth and morality in favor of a new vision—the will to power. Informed by both early Greco-Roman opponents of Christianity and modern European critics, and bringing unique criticisms of his own, his work has remained a worldwide focus of study. In *Ecce Homo*, his title takes Pontius Pilate's shocked exclamation upon seeing Jesus and audaciously and ironically turns those words to himself:

> I know my fate. One day my name will be associated with the memory of something tremendous—a crisis without equal on earth, the most profound collision of conscience, a decision that was conjured up against everything that had been believed, demanded, hallowed so far. I am no man, I am dynamite.[4]

Nietzsche's prophetic self-assessment was not far overstated. His life and work have remained a collision against the hallowed beliefs of faith.

There are multiple ways to approach Nietzsche's basic doctrines of the Übermensch (overman or superman), the will to power, the subversive moral and religious influence of the lower-class rabble, and eternal recurrence. But for understanding the roots of our contemporary religious situation, everything begins and ends with his unswerving rejection of God. What others said in a pedestrian manner, Nietzsche says with corrosive flair: "God is a thought that makes crooked all that is straight."[5] Employing erudite etymological analysis, acidic suspicion, ad hominem, and ribald mockery of everything Christian, Nietzsche launches what is quite possibly the most challenging attack that Christianity has ever faced. Our task is first to air his critique, and then to respond to this nineteenth-century endeavor in darkness.

The Rejection of God, Christ, and Transcendence in General

Throughout his adult life, Nietzsche was explicit about the nonexistence of God: "We deny God, we deny the responsibility in God: only thereby do we redeem the world."[6] This son and grandson of Lutheran pastors had come to see God as an elaborately developed fiction and belief in God "as miserable, as absurd, as harmful, not merely as an error but as a crime against life."[7] For Nietzsche, responsible thought and behavior begins with combat against Christianity, that "crime against life," and turns to Dionysian engagement of this godless world. Dionysus, Greek god of wine and fertility, could inspire his devotees to heightened achievement in art and literature. Like wine, Dionysus could bring ecstatic frenzy or fierce rage—which Nietzsche mirrors in his writing, especially in *Thus Spoke Zarathustra* (written and published in four parts, 1883–1885).[8]

In Nietzsche's *Zarathustra*, when the eponymous anti-prophet shouts, "Curse all cowardly devils in you who like to whine and fold their hands and pray," the people declare, "Zarathustra is godless." But Zarathustra proudly responds, "Yes, I am Zarathustra the godless!" Turning godlessness into lofty virtue, Zarathustra asks, "Who is more godless than I, that I may delight in his instruction?"[9] Zarathustra, an artistic rendition of Nietzsche's views, portrays a completely godless way to celebrate this world with Dionysian exuberance.

Nietzsche's venom against Christianity is unparalleled: "What was formerly just sick is today indecent—it is indecent to be a Christian today. . . . If we have even the smallest claim to integrity, we must know today that a theologian, a priest, a pope, not merely is wrong in every sentence he speaks, but lies."[10] The trajectory of Nietzsche's corpus is a counter-narrative performance against what he claims to be centuries of accumulated falsehood and deceit.

Belief in God is worse confounded by belief in Christ. Since Nietzsche denies that God exists, it follows that he also denies that Christ is God's Son. His title *The Antichrist* is deliberately provocative; Nietzsche takes literally the biblical meaning, "This is the antichrist, the one who denies the Father and the Son" (1 John 2:22); he owns it and scoffs at it. "Antichrist" is a title that Nietzsche is proud to claim.[11]

Mocking Jesus is a motif of Nietzsche's repertoire. Nietzsche despises Jesus' teachings that everyone is a child of the God that Nietzsche does not believe in.[12] He characterizes Jesus as "this most interesting of all decadents . . . a mixture of the sublime, the sickly, and the childlike."[13] Nietzsche has Zarathustra declare, "He whom they call Redeemer has put them in fetters: in fetters of false values and delusive words. Would that someone would yet redeem them from their Redeemer!"[14] In fact, Nietzsche's writings are a continuous attempt at this kind of "redemption."

When Zarathustra comes upon "The Voluntary Beggar," whose teachings bear some resemblance to Jesus', this Voluntary Beggar, this "sermonizer on the mount," is preaching to cows. When asked why he disturbs the cows, the Voluntary Beggar responds with words that contemptuously ridicule Jesus' phraseology and teachings. The vignette ends when Zarathustra refuses to accept the Voluntary Beggar's compliments and drives him away while threatening to beat him with a stick.[15] Nietzsche could not be clearer that peace between his worldview and Jesus' is not possible. Zarathustra later reiterates the point: "To be sure: except ye become as little children, ye shall not enter into that kingdom of heaven. (And Zarathustra pointed upward with his hands.) But we have no wish whatever to enter into the kingdom of heaven: we have become men—so we want the earth."[16] Nietzsche disavows Jesus' teachings with unrivaled vehemence.

Indeed, Nietzsche's rejection of God and Jesus expresses almost unimaginable insults: "The god on the cross is a curse on life."[17] Similarly, Nietzsche's Zarathustra insultingly twists Jesus' memorable words and historic actions at the Last Supper. At this final meal with his disciples—his friends—Jesus initiates a new kind of meal: the eucharistic communion that has spiritually fed believers ever since, bringing believers into communion with Christ and thereby into communion with one another. But in a mocking and crude parody of the Last Supper, Zarathustra holds his own festival of men and a braying ass. Turning Jesus' communion upside down, Zarathustra declares that all present should reenact it egoistically, "for your own sakes," and in remembrance of Zarathustra, the new prophet of godlessness.[18]

In addition to the blanket rejection of God and egregious mockery of Jesus, Nietzsche also denies every semblance of transcendence. There is no above; there is no other life. Thus Zarathustra implores, "I beseech you, my brothers, remain faithful to the earth, and do not believe those who speak to you of otherworldly hopes! Poison-mixers are they, whether they know it or not. Despisers of life are they, decaying and poisoned themselves, of whom the earth is weary: so let them go."[19] For Nietzsche, any looking beyond this life is the poison with which Christianity has infected so many cultures. All transcendence must be rejected as the worst kind of falsehood, a deliberate "spiritual" blindness that looks away from the world as it is.

The Rejection of Truth and Morality: Revaluation and Reversal

Revaluation of Truth

From Abraham to Jesus to the present day, Judaism and Christianity have been centrally concerned with truth about God, the created world, and ourselves. Jesus proclaims both that "you will know the truth, and the truth will make you free" (John 8:32) and that "when the Spirit of truth comes, he will guide you into all the truth" (John 16:13). In a momentous confrontation, Jesus tells his judge, Pontius Pilate, "For this I came into the world, to testify to the truth"—to which Pilate ironically and skeptically responds, "What is truth?" (John 18:37, 38). Nietzsche applauds Pilate's "noble scorn," finding Pilate to be the only respectable figure in the New Testament.[20]

In the absence of transcendence, "truth" becomes questionable; it can only be used with scare quotes. Nietzsche echoes Pilate's scornful question and provides an infamous challenge to the very possibility of truth:

> What, then, is truth? A mobile army of metaphors, metonyms, and anthropomorphisms—in short, a sum of human relations, which have been enhanced, transposed, and embellished poetically and rhetorically, and which after long use seem firm, canonical, and obligatory to a people: truths are illusions about which one has forgotten that this is what they are; metaphors which are worn out and without sensuous power; coins which have lost their pictures and now matter only as metal, no longer as coins.[21]

Contending that "truths are illusions," an "army of metaphors," demotes "truth" to historical fiction, socially sanctioned with a false aura of transcendence. This contention would pull the rug out from under human knowledge, leaving only an isolated will to perpetrate its preferences. Pontius Pilate could approach "truth" as a disposable frill because he represented the *power* of Rome. Anyone who doubted the reality of that power could be made to experience it in unforgettable ways.

But in our current day, many undergraduates have never read the biblical account of Jesus and Pilate's confrontation about truth. Breathing the relativistic air of our late modern period, many unwittingly follow Pilate in their inability to affirm that truth is universal. Not exactly skeptical, they tend to use "truth" with air quotes.

Genealogy, i.e. Nietzsche's historical analysis of how "truth" and "morality" came to be, is a tool of extreme suspicion. If there is no unchanging truth, its proponents must be exposed through genealogy as either ignorant or as liars and frauds, salesmen of the superstitious. Nietzsche contends that "after Christian truthfulness has drawn one inference after another, it must end by drawing its *most striking inference*, its inference *against* itself."[22] Nietzsche's targeting of truth against truth is dizzying; except for the pursuit of power, it leaves no foundation, neither external nor internal. Nietzsche believes that the future belongs to Pilate, not Jesus.

Against the centuries-old belief "that God is truth, that truth is divine," Nietzsche asks, "But what if . . . God himself turns out to be our longest lie?"[23] The Third Essay of *The Genealogy of Morals* (1887) is a protracted attack on faith in truth that Nietzsche had earlier anticipated: "There are many kinds of 'truths,' and consequently there is no truth."[24] Nietzsche's denial of truth leads him to his so-called perspectivism. Without a universal there can only be individual perspectives. Repudiating Kantian as well as Judeo-Christian universalism, Nietzsche contends that one must create his own virtue, goodness, and duty in order to foster his own power.[25] In the absence of truth, those who are able should openly exert the will to power, since claims of truth merely mask the underlying will to power.

Revaluation of Good and Evil

Denying the reality of God, Christ, transcendence, and truth, Nietzsche treats morality as an equally unreal corollary. In his account, morality has a nonmoral origin and history—the pointed edge of genealogy. Exploring etymologies and their concomitant histories, Nietzsche argues that from the distinction between noble and common people comes "the origin of the antithesis 'good' and 'bad.'"[26] "The good" referred to the "the noble, powerful, high-stationed and high-minded, who felt and established themselves and their actions as good, that is, of the first rank, in contradistinction to all the low, low-minded, common and plebeian."[27] In Greek, Latin, and German, Nietzsche finds repeated etymological evidence for his theory of the origin of good and bad, where "good" always referred to noble, and "bad" to common or plebeian.[28]

In Nietzsche's genealogical analysis, the weaker parties experienced *resentment* at their subordinate status (Nietzsche uses the French *ressentiment*); led by priests, they sought means to overcome their superiors through a sleight of hand—a revaluation of values. Nietzsche contends that the entire edifice of God, transcendence, truth, and morality is a fabrication, an invention born of the weak's resentment. Where the original distinction of conqueror/vanquished, noble/common, master/slave was between "good" and "bad," the decisive move of the impotent underclass was to introduce the distinction between "good" and "*evil*." The resentful underclass applies the new distinction to its own advantage—a sly maneuver to overpower the naturally powerful.[29]

With characteristic verve, Nietzsche illustrates the new meaning of evil. It makes sense that lambs do not like birds of prey that carry off little lambs: "And if the lambs say among themselves: 'these birds of prey are evil; and whoever is least like a bird of prey, but rather its opposite, a lamb—would he not be good?'"[30] Multiplying metaphors of disdain, Nietzsche portrays the resentful as "cellar rodents full of vengefulness and hatred," who turn weakness into something meritorious, impotence into goodness of heart, and natural lowliness of station into the virtue of humility. These resentful ones turn everything onto its head with inventions like "justice," "kingdom of God," "faith," "hope," and "love."[31]

In this genealogical view, traditional morality is an entirely made-up fiction by which the weak command the strong, as the priests, the embodiment of *ressentiment*, designate the harsh conquerors as evil. History, he contends, has been dominated by the priests, especially the Jewish priests, "the most evil enemies" whose impotence is compensated with the most "poisonous kind of hatred. . . . All that has been done on earth against the 'noble,' 'the powerful,' 'the masters,' 'the rulers,' fades into nothing compared with what the *Jews* have done against them."[32] The Jews successfully opposed enemy conquerors with their priestly values, a complete "revaluation of their enemies' values"—a history-shaping act of spiritual resentment and revenge.[33] In Nietzsche's analysis, Christianity is the inheritor of the Jewish, priestly morality; and Christian love is just an evolved form of *ressentiment*, a very successful graft onto the ancient Jewish tree.[34]

Where the original relation of master and slave was a function of nature, values are an artificial human creation, as Zarathustra proclaims, "Verily, men gave themselves all their good and evil. Verily, they did not take it, they did not find it, nor did it come to them as a voice from heaven."[35] Since values are neither discovered nor revealed by a god, Nietzsche calls for another reversal of values, one that is in accord with nature's determination of strong and weak. In his preface to *The Antichrist*, Nietzsche presents a "Revaluation of All Values"—his own revaluation, a reversal that would overturn Judeo-Christian morality:

> What is good? Everything that heightens the feeling of power in man, the will to power, power itself.
>
> What is bad? Everything that is born of weakness.
>
> What is happiness? The feeling that power is growing, that resistance is overcome.
>
> Not contentedness but more power; not peace but war; not virtue but fitness . . .[36]

Ridding ourselves of the phantoms of God and transcendence, good and evil must be redefined in terms of this world alone.

Nietzsche's redefinitions, so central to his worldview, are dramatically highlighted by Zarathustra: "Everything that the good call evil must come together so that one truth may be born. O my brothers, are you evil enough for this truth? The audacious daring, the long mistrust, the cruel No, the disgust, the cutting into the living—how rarely does all this come together. But from such seed is truth begotten."[37] Nietzsche's Zarathustra wants there to be more evil: "For evil is man's best strength. 'Man must become better and more evil'—thus I teach."[38] The strong must simply be willing to be strong, even if dominance requires harming or killing: "In great men, the specific qualities of life—injustice, falsehood, exploitation—are at their greatest."[39] Nietzsche's revaluation permeates his corpus. It is not rhetorical hyperbole; it is a radical redefinition that would overthrow the Christian worldview. Zarathustra removes any doubt about where it leads:

> The weak and the failures shall perish: first principle of our love of man. And they shall even be given every possible assistance.
>
> What is more harmful than any vice? Active pity for all the failures and all the weak: Christianity.[40]

Where Comte rejected Christianity but attempted to retain love for others, Nietzsche rejected such halfway measures. For Nietzsche love is neither a virtue nor a goal; it is merely an unreal remnant of priestly history, an undue obstruction to the rightful power of the Übermensch.

The Übermensch and the Will to Power

Nietzsche sees himself as godless but not as valueless. His sole value, however, is revaluation, the restoration of the Übermensch. The Übermensch has three tasks of overcoming. He must overcome the Christian lies about a nonexistent God with the associated fabrications of transcendence, truth, and morality; must overcome the rabble that produced these underhanded fictions; and through the disciplined, ascetic pursuit of the will to power, must continuously overcome and enhance himself.

Zarathustra teaches his hearers that just as the ape is "a laughingstock or a painful embarrassment" to man, so too is a mere man a laughingstock and embarrassment to the Übermensch.[41] The development of the Übermensch is Nietzsche's positive program, his response to the nihilism that he believes Christianity caused, first by perpetrating lies and then by collapsing in the Enlightenment and post-Enlightenment critiques. Thus Zarathustra declares,

> I teach the overman. Man is something that shall be overcome. . . . Behold, I teach you the overman. The overman is the meaning of the earth.[42]

The qualities and the morality of the Übermensch are vastly different from the Christian, because the Übermensch must "become hard." Becoming hard will "impress your hand on millennia as on wax . . . . Only the noblest is altogether hard."[43] Zarathustra insistently warns the would-be Übermensch against peace:

> You should have eyes that always seek an enemy—your enemy. . . . You should love peace as a means to new wars—and the short peace more than the long. To you I do not recommend work but struggle. To you I do not recommend peace but victory. Let your peace be a victory! . . .
>
> "What is good?" you ask. To be brave is good.[44]

Like the conquerors of old, in Nietzsche's *The Genealogy of Morals*, the Übermensch himself *is* the good. "Good" is not a universal, transcendent value; it is what the Übermensch does, what he is. He sets his own rules and establishes his own standards.

In the revealing title *Beyond Good and Evil* (1886), Nietzsche lays out additional qualities of the overman:

> Here we must beware of superficiality and get to the bottom of the matter, resisting all sentimental weakness: Life itself is *essentially* appropriation, injury, overpowering of what is alien and weaker; suppression, hardness, imposition of one's own forms, incorporation and at least, at its mildest, exploitation . . .[45]

Sentimentality is a vestige of the false picture of Judeo-Christian claims about God and humankind. The strength of the overman includes the strength to overcome what others, especially Christians, may sentimentally believe.

The overman must be contemptuous of the rabble, the commoner, whom Zarathustra designates as the "last man." These last men have petty concerns, like happiness, comfort, and pleasure.[46] Against "shopkeepers" who seek to be good neighbors as they seek trivial things, Zarathustra wants people who will say, "'I want to be master—over peoples.' . . . the best should rule, the best also want to rule."[47] The virtue of the overman is *egoism*, not altruism. Zarathustra advocates loving oneself wholeheartedly, and he sneers at the teaching to love the neighbor as perpetrating "the best lies and hypocrisies." In a complete reversal of Jesus' call to love all people, those who teach love of neighbor are called "a grave burden for all the world."[48] Nietzsche wholly denies the sense of justice that Christianity bequeathed on the world, as Zarathustra proclaims, "I do not wish to be mixed up and confused with these preachers of equality. For, to me justice speaks thus: 'Men are not equal.' Nor shall they become equal! What would my love of the overman be if I spoke otherwise?"[49] Nietzsche's repugnance toward Christian justice and its offshoots, even heretical offshoots, is consistent. He is repulsed both by socialist advocacy for the "herd animal" and by Immanuel Kant, whom he denigrates as "an underhanded Christian" and "the very recipe for decadence, even for idiocy."[50] Nietzsche relentlessly attacks any religion, moral philosophy, and political or economic movement that empowers the weak and restrains the strong.

The Übermensch in Context: The Natural World as the Never-Ending Will to Power

As Nietzsche affirms the Übermensch as "the meaning of the world," and as he denies God, transcendence, truth, and morality, he also presents an unusual view of the natural world, one that blends Dionysian mythology, a nineteenth-century understanding of the conservation of energy, and a strong sense of struggle (without adopting Darwinian evolution). What Nietzsche could not abide is the Judeo-Christian doctrine of creation, in which nature is intentionally brought into being and then moves through a developmental history toward its final purpose—human union with God.

Rejecting the notion of a created beginning to the universe, Nietzsche joins the ancient Greek view of time as cyclic, with a universe that is "a monster of energy, without beginning, without end; a firm, iron magnitude of force that does not grow bigger or smaller, that does not expend itself but only transforms itself . . ."[51] What Nietzsche refuses to believe, that God is "without beginning and without end," he chooses to believe about nature. In his view, the universe is entirely naturalistic, "a monster of energy," where all is an endless stream of strife and occasional harmony, a realm of becoming for both nature and humanity ensconced therein. Like Comte, Nietzsche seeks to avoid first and last things. But where Comte is agnostic about such things and thinks that seeking them leads to futility, Nietzsche's cyclical view of time implies that there are no first or last things.

Through Zarathustra, Nietzsche portrays his ultimate context, the eternal recurrence of the same: "Everything goes, everything comes back; eternally rolls the wheel of being. Everything dies, everything blossoms again; eternally runs the year of being. . . . eternally the same house of being is being built."[52] In this cosmology, time and all things within time are cyclic; they return again and again. Zarathustra's talking animals thus acclaim him, "You are the teacher of the eternal recurrence—that is your destiny! . . . that all things recur eternally, and we ourselves too; and that we have already existed an eternal number of times, and all things with us."[53] Nietzsche sees the eternal recurrence of everything "as a becoming that knows no satiety, no disgust, no weariness; this, my *Dionysian* world of the eternally self-creating, the eternally self-destroying . . . . *This world is the will to power—and nothing besides!* And you yourselves are also this will to power—and nothing besides!"[54] The overall context is surging with creation and destruction in a manner fitting with the creative destructivity of the Übermensch. The Übermensch is the one who enters into the hardness of the world and joyfully exerts his own hardness. The Übermensch, having divested himself of all tales of God, truth, and morality, must learn to joyfully will each moment, because each moment will eternally return.

Nietzsche is haunted by eternity. Having rejected a transcendent eternity, he struggles to construct one that is immanent. Like many of the ancient Greeks, he assumes an eternal world; and he declares with some bravado, "We need not worry for a moment about the hypothesis of a *created* world."[55] But he does need to worry about how the Übermensch confronts the repetitive cosmology, where everything, every deed, thought, and event is repeated: "My formula for greatness in a human being is *amor fati*: that one wants nothing to be different, not forward, not backward, not in all eternity. Not merely bear what is necessary, still less conceal it . . . but love it."[56] The Übermensch who is the "the meaning of the earth" must learn to love himself and his deeds—to will all that he does as a punctuation within the eternal recurrence. Thus part 3 of *Zarathustra* ends with a sevenfold refrain:

> Never yet have I found the woman from whom I wanted children, unless it be this woman whom I love: for I love you, O eternity.
> *For I love you, O eternity!*[57]

In Nietzsche's strange cosmology, each act is a begetting—one that lives forever and is forever repeated.

Nietzsche is not troubled that the constant flux of cause and effect dissolves both person and soul. As Zarathustra teaches, "The soul is as mortal as the body. But the knot of causes in which I am entangled recurs and will create me again. I myself belong to the causes of the eternal recurrence. I come again, with this sun, with this earth . . . not to a new life or a better life or a similar life: I come back eternally to this same, selfsame life."[58] Since each person is merely a "knot of causes" in nature's cycle of never-ending creations and destructions, then the "soul," which smacks of transcendence, must be reduced to the body: "Body am I entirely, and nothing else; and soul is only a word for something about the body."[59] In this naturalistic picture, all is reduced to the whirl of nature: "soul" is reduced to the body; and the body is part of the causation of the whirl. But the Übermensch plays his role joyfully.

Nietzsche and the Reich: Nietzsche Used and Abused

In "Nietzsche's Political Misappropriation," Tracy Strong argues that "Nietzsche is available to a wide range of political appropriations, indeed perhaps to all."[60] Nietzsche is especially vulnerable to misappropriation because he so often went in two different directions: he centrally argued that Judaism and its Christian offshoot had swindled superior peoples; yet he repeatedly denounced both anti-Semitism and German nationalism. He celebrated war and despised peace, but he opposed the growing power of Prussia in his time.

Nietzsche's sweeping denial of Christianity had to produce collateral damage. His accusation that the Apostle Paul's views were not only false, but also mendacious, was couched in explosive terms: "And once more the priestly instinct of the Jew committed the same great crime against history."[61] The problem is that the designation, "the priestly instinct of the Jew," and the accusation, "the same great crime against history," were ready-to-use explosives for those already disposed to disdain Jews. Nietzsche's scattershot critique struck more than just Paul. His slur upon Christianity was intertwined with a claim of centuries of Jewish lying: "In Christianity all of Judaism, a several-century-old Jewish preparatory training and technique of the most serious kind, attains its ultimate mastery as the art of lying in a holy manner. The Christian, this *ultima ratio* of the lie, is the Jew once more—even three times more."[62] Accusing Christians of embodying and intensifying what he characterizes as the basic *Jewish* lie is recklessly inciteful; it makes misappropriation easy and gives it plausibility.

Had Nietzsche lived to see the rise of National Socialism (they took power thirty-three years after his death), he might very well have opposed it. Nonetheless, the National Socialists readily adopted Nietzsche's central themes of Übermensch, will to power, validation of cruelty, greatness and destiny, strength, ruthlessness, and preference for war.[63] At the beginning of World War II, the Nazis distributed 150,000 copies of *Zarathustra* to their troops.[64] The inflammatory rhetoric, the repudiation of the West's allegiance to truth and morality, and the call for the hard power of the Übermensch were irresistible fodder for the Reich.

Not only in World War II, but already in World War I, Nietzsche was blamed for fomenting international mayhem. Along with the German nationalist Heinrich von Treitschke, French Catholic clergy held Nietzsche responsible for "Germany's amoral bellicosity." When a new English translation of Nietzsche's works appeared during the war, one Piccadilly bookshop advertised, "The Euro-Nietzschean War. Read the Devil in order to fight him better."[65] These responses to Nietzsche were extreme and did not take into account offsetting parts of Nietzsche's writings. However, during a war of destruction and death on a scale never before encountered, it is hardly surprising that subtlety suffered. While Nietzsche opposed nationalism, especially *German* nationalism, his works were bellicose and amoral. For example, in an oft-cited passage, Nietzsche wrote,

> For what is freedom? . . . That one is prepared to sacrifice human beings for one's cause, not excluding oneself. Freedom means that the manly instincts which delight in war and victory dominate over other instincts, for example, over those of "pleasure." The human being who has *become free*—and how much more the *spirit* who has become free—spits on the contemptible type of well-being dreamed of by shopkeepers, Christians, cows, females, Englishmen, and other democrats. The free man is a *warrior*.[66]

Nietzsche attempted something massive—conceptual war that would reverse millennia of Christianity and its associated morality. In the actual combat of the Franco-Prussian War (1870–1871), Nietzsche took leave from his university post and volunteered for dangerous service at the front, where he evacuated the dead and wounded from the battlefield. In later years, in spite of extreme physical duress, headache, intestinal cramps, vomiting, and insomnia, Nietzsche was unrelenting in his conceptual war. He had little understanding of and even less respect for English contentedness and moderation.

On the other hand, Nietzsche's writings also make it clear that he was no German nationalist: "It is part of my ambition to be considered a despiser of the Germans *par excellence*. . . . When I imagine a type of man that antagonizes all my instincts, it always turns into a German."[67] Additionally, Nietzsche treated Treitschke and his stridently nationalist views with considerable sarcasm.[68] In *Zarathustra*, Nietzsche characterized the glorification of the state as a new idolatry.[69] A modern nation-state, after all, would include mostly rabble. And yet, his elsewhere stated preference for war to peace and praise of the Roman imperium and the ancient Greeks at war were easily (mis) appropriated by those who did glorify the state. It seems that there are always ways to argue both sides in this controversy about Nietzsche.

Whatever the nuances, Nietzsche's opposition to anti-Semitism was clear. At Christmas 1887, he wrote to his sister, "Your association with an anti-Semitic chief [her husband] expresses a foreignness to my whole way of life which fills me again and again with ire or melancholy. . . . that the name of Zarathustra is used in every *Anti-Semitic Correspondence Sheet*, has almost made me sick several times."[70] Nietzsche also sought a new publisher, calling his old one "an anti-Semitic dump."[71] Accusing Germans of being "vulgar" and incapable of grasping his meaning, he adds, "From Jews, yes; never yet from Germans."[72] Nietzsche's utter disgust at Judaism-become-Christianity did not include hatred of Jews. He praised "their energy and higher intelligence" and contended that "as soon as it is no longer a matter of preserving nations, but of producing the strongest possible European mixed race, the Jew is just as useful and desirable as any other national remnant."[73] Nietzsche's opposition to anti-Semitism was reasoned, consistent, and sincere.

But the distinction between Nietzsche's anti-Judaism and racial anti-Semitism was all too easily lost on the anti-Semites of his time and on those who would succeed them, a blurring that Nietzsche himself helped to occur: "To gain that tremendous energy of greatness in order to shape the man of the future through breeding and, on the other hand, the annihilation of millions of failures, and not to perish of the suffering one creates, though nothing like it has ever existed!—"[74] For those who did seek great conquest and "the annihilation of millions," Nietzsche's words could be selectively chosen like low-hanging fruit.

That Nietzsche would be appropriated by anti-Semitic politicians is at least partially due to his own teaching and the extreme rhetoric with which he delivered it. But extreme politics—it matters little whether of left or right—is a predictable outcome of the denial of transcendence so central in Nietzsche's thought. No one was more vehement in the denial of transcendence than Friedrich Nietzsche. And no one directly attacked belief in God and mocked Jesus Christ with anything like Nietzsche's unrestrained hostility. When Zarathustra boasts, "Who is more godless than I, that I may delight in his instruction?" Nietzsche may have won the prize for godlessness.[75] However, the recipient of that kind of prize may have attracted fellow travelers not to his liking.

For those who believe that God does not exist and that truth is a matter of one's own perspective, politics tends to become weightier, even though Nietzsche himself never fell prey to this tendency. To the unbeliever, God is a fable; and to fainthearted believers, God seems a rather distant and uninvolved being. But the lure of politics is that it seems close and bigger than individual life, and political effects are often demonstrable and immediate. Yet any political program that fails to sincerely recognize something more important than politics will come to grief, because its solely immanental structure is not strong enough to bear the stresses of human activity and the irrepressible quest for human meaning. When politics is the highest reality, it becomes the will to power writ large, opponents inevitably become enemies, and history has taught us to expect paroxysms of disappointment, disillusion, pain, and organized violence. The denial of transcendence can be sophisticated or crass, but in its wake, gravitational implosion is likely.

Counter-Assessments

> As for me and my household, we will serve the Lord.
> **Josh 24:15**

If the manger of Bethlehem did not host the Son of God incarnate, if Jesus was just another child born to a captive people in a distant Roman province, then Nietzsche's extended diatribe against Christianity would not be unjustified. But if Jesus was the God-man, truly divine and truly human, then Nietzsche assaulted the most beautiful, noble, and gracious gift ever given, and set his life's work against

Jesus' teachings of hope and enduring love for all of humankind—the strong, the average, and the weak. Nietzsche hated the concept, but he at least understood the claim that in Christ all humankind is unified as the family of God (Gal 3:28).

The Possibilities of This World: Transcendence and Immanence

At its best, Christianity has never been a pale, one-sided concern with transcendence. The genius of the faith, which stems from the divine and human dual status of its incarnate founder, has always linked transcendence to immanence, joining heaven and earth through pathways that the incarnate Christ established and continues to foster. Christ's promise of a life to come in no way devalues this current life with which Nietzsche is so exclusively concerned. Additionally, the doctrine of creation ex nihilo, rather than devaluing earthly life, is profoundly world-affirming—an announcement of the goodness of creation. Believing that the universe is intentionally created sparks a sense of awe, a deep appreciation of sheer givenness, and a fundamental orientation within and love for this initial universe home. And when we leave this home, we will not be circling back toward it, but rather toward eternal delights that "no eye has seen, nor ear heard, nor the human heart conceived" (1 Cor 2:9). By contrast, Nietzsche's endless recurrence of the same looks like eternal house arrest.

Because in creation and in Christ the Christian sense of transcendence is so tied to immanence, Nietzsche's allegation of otherworldliness is a misrepresentation, a straw man. He essentially accuses Christianity of the Gnosticism and Manicheanism that it has rejected since the second century. The Gnostics (c. AD 140) were the first heretics because they denied the goodness of creation. Seeking an "otherworldly" escape is a violation of Christian thought and practice. Our expectation of another and better world should increase our love for and effectiveness in this world. Uniquely, Christianity's joining of transcendence and immanence is an addition of spiritual power for this life, and not at all a disavowal.

Where Nietzsche proclaims that "the weak and the failures shall perish," and that their Christian support is "more harmful than any vice," he again misrepresents.[76] A mature Christian love does not leave people wallowing in failure, but instead offers an awakening to life, dignity, and transformation. Those transformed by Christian love have done much to transform their communities. Historically, the widespread advance of Christian faith has also led to social, economic, and political development, not through the will to power and conquest, but rather through civility and peace.

The dispute with Nietzsche can take on sophisticated airs, but it is not determined by demonstrations of reason or aesthetics; for both Nietzsche and Christianity everything rests on a basic belief about where this world comes from and what its basic purpose is. While I always enjoy meeting outstanding individuals, Nietzsche's claim that "the overman is the meaning of the earth" is not a particularly impressive proposal.[77]

The Human Person

Since its inception, Christianity has been concerned about the human *person*. Taking its lead from the Jewish scripture, Christianity has seen all human persons as eternally valuable, being made in the image of God (Gen 1:26-27). Completely opposing this Christian respect for all, Nietzsche's hero worship of the Übermensch and his disdain for common people took a fatal turn in the wrong direction, a counsel of contempt prone to violence. His attempted deconstruction of the human person was likewise a move in the wrong direction, reducing person and soul to nature alone and human nature to a "knot of [natural] causes." Having so thoroughly flattened things, Nietzsche advocated that the strong enthusiastically enter into conflict, exerting the will to power over others—all of which David Bentley Hart has humorously characterized as "his rather adolescent adoration of pagan harshness."[78] Looking askance at Nietzsche's "seemingly unreflective naturalism," Hart contends that "one might justly wonder whether the life he celebrates is anything more diverting than the upward thrusting of an empty will . . ."[79] Without transcendence or a soul to experience it, Nietzsche's view of a human person is empty bang and bluster.

Just as Nietzsche would empty the human person of substance, he also negates the morality that distinguishes humans from other animals. His anti-Christian alternative to morality is a call for "splendid animality"—yet another naturalistic flattening; and his call for "instincts that delight in war and conquest" have not been unheeded, but they have been disastrous.[80]

Nietzsche's own life became a lived contradiction between the hardness of his published views and the gentle love whose absence was so hard to bear. Nietzsche made several marriage proposals, all of which the women were wise enough to reject. In his last years before the onset of insanity, Nietzsche was highly productive but extremely lonely and unhappy, as revealed in his letter to Peter Gast, January 15, 1888: "There are nights in which I can no longer endure myself; it is thoroughly humiliating."[81] Likewise, in a letter to Franz Overbeck, February 3, 1888, a "black despair" had set upon him, and he lamented the "perpetual lack of a truly refreshing and healing human love, the absurd isolation it involves and the fact that any remaining connection to people only causes afflictions."[82] Nietzsche had been very close friends with the older Richard Wagner, but Nietzsche became highly critical of Wagner's redemption through art and repeatedly published stinging criticisms. The dissolution of the friendship undoubtedly affected Wagner, who had earlier told Nietzsche, "Strictly speaking, you are the only benefit apart from my wife that life has brought my way."[83] The loss of the friendship greatly weighed on Nietzsche, who wrote in a letter to Peter Gast, "It strikes me as so foolish to insist on being right at the expense of love."[84] Yet Nietzsche did insist, and Wagner and his wife Cosima were appalled by the public criticism in *Human, All Too Human*. As Cosima wrote, "I know that evil has triumphed here."[85] The break was irreparable. As the years drew on, Nietzsche still had friends like Gast and Overbeck, but he was increasingly isolated. Bereft of human love, Nietzsche drew ever closer to madness. On January 3, 1889, Nietzsche observed a carriage driver beating his horse. Nietzsche threw his arms around the horse's mane and wept uncontrollably, the last conscious act of the portrayer of the Übermensch. He spent his remaining years in asylums in mostly catatonic incoherence.

From the aggrieved little boy who had lost his father and then his little brother, to the radical genius experiencing great physical suffering and "black despair," Nietzsche's life was never easy. But whatever difficulties must be faced, beliefs and worldview affect relations and the tenor of our lives. At least to some degree, Nietzsche was an early victim of his own views.

A Distorted View of Eternity

Nietzsche's doctrine of the eternal recurrence of the same is the very antithesis of the grace of creation and a futile attempt to immanentize eternity within time. Nietzsche asks us to believe in a myth that long ago did battle with and was defeated by the Christian narrative of creation and Christ. Except perhaps for overwrought philologists, the old Dionysian myth has no more power now than it had in the first centuries after Christ; Nietzsche's nineteenth-century Dionysian vision of eternal return is not an advancement on the defeated first-century vision. By contrast, the Christian story of divine creation as gift has lost none of its life-giving power; it was and is the superior narrative—even for the strongest of men. In the first three centuries after Christ, the victory of the Christian vision was in large part due to understanding this life as a divine *gift*, an inherently creative creation that calls forth wonder, gratitude, and cooperation—an infinitely superior choice to a puerile celebration of conflict and dominance. While one can always find skeptical explanations for historical developments, it is at least possible that a development wins against its competitors because it is true.

Karl Löwith, one of the premier interpreters of modern German philosophy, argues that Nietzsche did not and could not successfully reconcile eternal recurrence of the same and the will to power.[86] Since there is a finite number of possible states of the world and there is alleged to be infinite time, each state of the world, and each human choice, must recur and recur eternally. In this cosmic wheel of repetition, the Übermensch is supposed to will each action as something he can eternally affirm. The problem is that, if everything is recurring, then the freedom of the willing is nullified, because everything would already be repetition and thereby predestined. Hence, the best that one can do is to embrace fate (*amor fati*), because it will happen no matter what. There is something almost comical about trying to enclose eternity within time and space, with masters and slaves quarreling in the back seat as the universe rides in an eternal cycle of repetition.

In music and in most of life, there is good repetition and bad repetition. The high point of the classical symphony's sonata form, for example, is the recapitulation, the point at which the conflicted harmony of the development section ends and the original melody *returns* in the original key. At the recapitulation the repetition is exciting and fresh; it re-presents the old melody in a new way. But Nietzsche's eternal return is always the return of the same—done the same way, experienced the same way. Nietzsche's eternal recurrence of the same, were it ever to occur, would be more likely to produce a hellish ennui. Nietzsche's attempt to sequester eternity into time ends up being the most dreadful repetition of the same. It glimpses the beauty of creation and then turns its back on creation's ever-renewing development and freshness. Time has an important relation to eternity, but not because time is eternal; time is intensely valuable because it allows a unique, unrepeatable history—first inorganic, then organic, and finally, human persons conscious of time, the natural world, ourselves—and God.

Reconsidering Strength

In Nietzsche's telling, strength and power are good and weakness is bad—a rather simplistic affirmation of the obvious. By contrast, the Christian understanding of strength and power is complex, multifaceted, and multileveled, as highlighted in Jesus' role reversals: "The greatest among you will be your servant" (Matt 23:11); "Whoever wants to be first must be last of all and servant of all" (Mark 9:35; cf. Matt 18:1-4; Luke 9:46-48). These role reversals have revealed new levels and new kinds of strength. Following Jesus, the strong who serve others have not in the least diminished their own strength. Keeping natural strength in reserve, they have found a new and subtler strength, a spiritual strength still aware of natural conflict and contest, but a strength that moves all involved to a higher level. Nietzsche begins and ends his career in suspicion, by believing that there is no higher level. His attempt to reverse Jesus' reversal is a denial of beauty and a recipe for unlimited human pain and unhappiness.

As we saw above, Nietzsche's monochrome view of strength leads him to scoff at "preachers of equality. For to me justice speaks thus: 'Men are not equal.' Nor shall they become equal! What would my love of the overman be if I spoke otherwise?"[87] But here again Nietzsche misrepresents, because he fails to recognize a basic distinction of Christian thought: the difference between spiritual equality before God and inequality in virtually every other respect. Nietzsche's bombastic attack depends upon conflating the distinction. For all of its bravado, the attack is no more than an enfeebled straw-man argument.

How we use whatever strength we may have is indicative of character, because as Nietzsche knew, strength has options that weakness does not have. Nietzsche, who so often sees and capitalizes on unusual possibilities, in this case sees only the narrow obvious that strength should be for the strong. In sharp contrast, Christ asks us to use strength for others, for love. With tragic results for his own life, and for those who have followed his teachings, Nietzsche thought that strength and love constituted an either/or.

There is another unusual strength in the courage to let go of error, a strengthening humility that not all our choices are right. Humility, which is decidedly not part of the program of the Übermensch, is a divine technique, a predisposition toward ongoing growth in knowledge, wisdom, love, and strength. Being wrong can weigh on the human soul.[88] Letting go of a mistake is accompanied by a lightening, a release, and a surge of happiness.

• • •

Few writers have been as influential as Nietzsche, whose work is read and discussed on every continent. Nietzsche's frontal assault on Christianity is now standard fare in universities. He inspired a generation of prominent writers, such as Thomas Mann; Ernst Bertram; Henri Bergson; the Third Reich's ideologue Alfred Baeumler, who wrote *Nietzsche: The Philosopher and Politician* (English translation, 1931); and a slew of postmodern writers from Jacques Derrida to Michel Foucault, who typically credit Nietzsche as the font of their work. Reinhard Hütter has observed the pervasive Nietzschean influence at work: "The epistemological skepticism and ontological nihilism implicit in his rigorous exercise of suspicion have become the unexamined conventional wisdom of the intellectual class that occupies the so-called humanities in countless college and university faculties."[89] Nietzsche's views and his methods are now part of the intellectual atmosphere of late modernity.

Nietzsche prophetically saw the turbulence, confusion, and wars of a civilization built on Judeo-Christian principles that it no longer believed in. But Nietzsche was not a mere diagnostician; his vehement, scornful atheism continues to contribute to and shape contemporary attitudes and beliefs.

We live in a complex age characterized by a perplexing array of possibilities, in which there are few norms and virtually none that are uncontested. Fundamental choices and orientations are no longer cultural, political, and religious presuppositions. No longer given with the life into which each one awakens, basic choices and orientation now require our own contemplation and intuition. But basic orientations can lean toward darkness or light, defeat or victory, death or life. In the last words of his last book, Nietzsche laid out a binary choice, "Dionysus versus the Crucified."[90] But the Hebrew Deuteronomist also saw the binary choice: "I have set before you life and death. . . . Choose life so that you and your descendants may live" (Deut 30:19).

CONCLUSION

The Broken and the Whole

> We shall never save civilisation as long as civilisation is our main object. We must learn to want something else even more.
>
> **C. S. Lewis**

> If Christian precepts prevail, the respective classes will not only be united in the bonds of friendship, but also in those of brotherly love. For they will understand and feel that all men are children of the same common Father, who is God.
>
> **Leo XIII**[1]

In the *Cratylus*, one of Plato's lesser known works, Socrates considers a shuttle on a weaving loom, how the carpenter originally conceived it and then built it according to his idea. But Socrates then asks, "And suppose the shuttle to be broken in making. Will he make another, looking to the broken one? Or will he look to the form according to which he made the other?"[2]

The previous chapters have portrayed a narrative of brokenness, the progressive shattering of the West's foundations. In "Critical Turns," we considered the intramural strife of the Reformation, the severity and breadth of Enlightenment criticism, and the French Revolution's rise and calamitous fall. In "Descent into Darkness," we examined Feuerbach's publicly avowed atheism, the Romantics' expression of extreme individualism, and then nihilism, anarchism, and the crushing devastation that Marxism wrought. And in the final two chapters we examined Comte's anti-theistic positivism and Nietzsche's scornful rejection of God and transcendence. Like Plato's carpenter, we have noted the brokenness, but we must now look again at what can restore human function and wholeness—the task of this concluding chapter.

While many renowned figures moved away from faith, there were numerous men and women who resisted trends of dissolution with devotion and creativity. Among the multitude that might be mentioned are musicians like Johann Sebastian Bach and George Frideric Handel, who produced a treasure trove of music that continues to inspire people on every continent. The Catholic Church of the sixteenth century, awakened from its lethargy, was led forward by a remarkable series of women and men,[3] and took on the effort at ecclesial reform at the Council of Trent (1545–1563). In eighteenth-century England, while Charles Wesley wrote hymns that are still sung around the world, his brother John Wesley revitalized the faith of tens of thousands, especially in the lower classes. Equally important, Wesley organized Methodist societies that provided practical aid to those in need. Many historians credit John Wesley with helping England to avoid the kind of revolution that arose in France and bringing about "something like an Enlightenment for the common man."[4] Wesley and his good friend William Wilberforce steadfastly fought to abolish slavery. And in the nineteenth century, while Byron and Goethe were flirting with the demonic, Dostoevsky was writing *The Demons*, a work exposing the depredations and spiritual ugliness of proto-revolutionary atheistic cells in Russia. Like Nietzsche, Dostoevsky recognized that something was terribly wrong, but unlike Nietzsche, Dostoevsky saw faith in Christ as the solution, not as the problem.

For all the increasingly open attacks on Christianity and its founder, countless millions continued to live in faith, trusting that their lives were laden with meaning and eternal value—the Christian conception of the unbroken whole. Events of divine/human cooperation are normally hidden, unreported in any written history, as the church and the gospel of Christ quietly proceed through the centuries. Jerome K. Williams points to a pattern: "The great works of God are inaugurated by and founded on the hidden battles and loving obedience of chosen individuals."[5] These are the people, and they are present in every age, who transcend their Zeitgeist; a few become well-known; most remain relatively obscure. In a letter to his son Michael, who was fighting at the front during World War II,

J. R. R. Tolkien encouraged him to remember the hidden nature of providence: "The future is impenetrable especially to the wise, . . . for what is really important is always hid from contemporaries, and the seeds of what is to be are quietly germinating in the dark in some forgotten corner."[6] Divine activity on behalf of and in cooperation with humanity has never ceased. Our age is anything but monolithic, but within its multiplicity are countless souls as enlivened by the gospel of Christ as were his first followers in the first century.

In the Context of Eternity

If I live in a city at peace, I can drive to work, purchase goods, or visit friends when I please. But if I live in a city under attack, I can leave home only with considerable forethought and strategy about safety. Context is in many ways determinative. To understand the purpose and value of life requires an understanding of its greater context. The dreariness of nihilism sees no greater context than this material universe and hence can detect neither value nor purpose. The joyful hope of Christianity first sees space, time, matter, and energy as elements of a divinely intended creation, a universe home fit for transcendent human activity; and it then sees the entirety of the universe, all of creation, as nested in eternity.

Seeing ourselves in the context of eternity casts a certain light on the events and import of life, orients us toward a purpose worthy of being everlasting, and in this orientation provides an organizing principle for thought, belief, and conduct. As C. S. Lewis put it,

> A continual looking forward to the eternal world is not . . . a form of escapism or wishful thinking, but one of the things a Christian is meant to do. It does not mean that we are to leave the present world as it is. . . . the Christians who did the most for the present world were just those who thought most of the next.[7]

We should love our nation and our culture, but we must do so as those who love even more something higher and greater. Paradoxically, those whose first love is the eternal kingdom of God are, in accord with their particular gifts, also those best equipped to love and serve this present world.

Immanuel Kant also recognized that, in order to support his quest for endless progress, he needed to postulate both God and the immortality of the soul. His analysis of the moral law led him to conclude that within time, morality, "the first and principal part of the highest good," would necessarily remain incomplete. Kant thus postulated God and the immortality of the soul "since this problem can be solved only in eternity."[8] I would add that in addition to the problem of morality, every vital question of human identity will either sink toward nihilist resignation, revolutionary utopianism, or find its solution in the greater context of eternity.

From the stoning of Stephen (Acts 7:54-60) to our own time, Christians confident of their eternal standing with God have displayed exemplary courage when forced to choose between truth and death. Sir Thomas More (1478–1535) had excelled in service of his king and country. But when Henry VIII demanded that he sign the Law of Succession, More preferred prison to affirming a law that would disrupt the unity of the church. Thomas Howard, the Duke of Norfolk, pleaded with his friend More to sign the king's Law of Succession and thereby save his life: "I would wish you somewhat to incline to the King's pleasure. For by God's body, Mr. More, 'the wrath of the king is death!'" "Is that all, my Lord?" responded Thomas. "Then there is no more difference between your Grace and me, but that I shall die today and you tomorrow."[9] Put to the test, immense numbers of Christians have loved truth and goodness more than living a longer stretch of time. From the outset, Jesus and then Paul were eminently clear about the created origin and eternal destiny of human life. As Paul declared, "If for this life only we have hoped in Christ, we are of all people most to be pitied" (1 Cor 15:19).

Eternity and History

History is a phenomenon in the middle; neither entirely random nor utterly determined, history is an intensively humanized realm of thought, action, and response. Each of us is both child and parent of history.[10] It consists of the entire spectrum of human activity, its uncountable events of friendship, happiness, and kindness, along with massive and tragic derailments like the Thirty Years War, the Terror of the French Revolution, and the hideous oppression of the Soviet gulag. In freedom, for good and ill, the actions of individuals and societies are sealed as concretized footprints in the historical flow.

Christianity can never retreat from history because Christianity is rooted in an historical event—the incarnation of the Son of God: "When the fullness of time had come, God sent his Son, born of a woman, born under the law" (Gal 4:4). Paul's reflection indicates a kind of divine patience, a strategic plan that awaits "the fullness of time," the historical point of readiness. Here again context is crucial. The incarnation only occurs after many centuries of development within Judaism, so that the events of Jesus' life and his teachings can presuppose the sturdy base of Hebrew monotheism. Additionally, the Pax Romana made the world safer than perhaps ever before, safety necessary for the extensive travel that word-of-mouth evangelization would require.

The twofold nature of the incarnate Son—truly God and truly man, truly divine and truly human—is the pivotal pattern, the starting point and foundation of Christian thought. As the divine Son is "born of a woman, born under the law," eternity penetrates time and redirects the flow of history. Human history is transformed by the incarnation, because, having hosted the divine Son, history is no longer merely human. While God has always worked with human beings to accomplish his purposes, the seal of incarnation establishes new possibilities. Once the Son of God entered human history, subjected himself to its laws, and fully participated in the flow of its events, history has in a radically new way become the divine Son's history—a shared enterprise between humanity and God.

Elevated by the life, teachings, death, and resurrection of the fully human and fully divine Son, history has ever since carried the sacred potential of divine/human cooperation. The sacred potential is available to communities, especially the church; and it is present in every individual life. Every human life not only has a history but actually is a history. If the nihilists were right, it would not matter how well or poorly any one person or the society as a whole happened to live. But if God created this world, lived in it, and died on a cross in it, then the potentially sacred history of each person becomes clear, the responsibility and privilege of human life come into focus. Wherever love, mercy, and forgiveness are shared, whenever the Word of the gospel is spoken and heard, a reenactment of the divine/human partnership occurs. Such reenactments, though they be unknown to the wider society, do not leave the world as it was.

While the church has often been marred by error and sin, it has played a key role in the ongoing history of divine/human cooperation. As Jerome Williams puts it, "An essential aspect of the Church as founded by Christ is that it is both a divine and human institution. This combination of humanity and divinity, a mixture that has often been found offensive to spiritually sensitive people, is God's preferred mode of artistry."[11] The divine artist is evidently willing to work with flawed people, families, and communities, and over time bring them to a more excellent state. Just as Aquinas observed that "grace does not destroy nature but perfects it,"[12] so too grace neither destroys history nor consumes it. Among those alert to the possibilities of cooperation with God, grace punctuates history, lifts it to meaningful new heights, and redirects it to a better future.

Transcendence and Immanence

In accord with the twofold nature of the incarnate Son, the Christian Weltanschauung is twofold—a vision of interactive transcendence and immanence. In the struggles unleashed by the Reformation, all sides maintained some version of the twofold vision. But from the earliest times of the Enlightenment to the present, more and more people have first denied the existence of God, and then denied that anything transcends the world and its material universe.

The denial of transcendence has unsurprisingly led to a flattened view of the human person and society. The dissemination of this view has affected millions of individuals and permeated every aspect of the West's (and now the world's) politics, economics, and education. As Reinhard Hütter summarizes, "The ideological premises of secularism were honed in the sixteenth and seventeenth centuries, became politically and socially explicit in the eighteenth century, imperial in the nineteenth and the first half of the twentieth century, and global in the second half of the twentieth and the early twenty-first century."[13] This secularized view of things a priori rules out divine activity in human affairs. Like Auguste Comte's positivism, it is both a material belief and an epistemology. Dogmatically committed to the denial of transcendence, secularists of a positivist bent have falsely inferred that great advances in science and technology mean that only scientific knowing is valid.

Nietzsche, who was vehement in his denial of transcendence, was at least clear about where the denial leads: "We no longer derive man from 'the spirit' or the 'deity'; we have placed him back among the animals."[14] The chasm between the secularist and Christian perspectives means that clashes are inevitable. Those who see themselves as "back among the animals" are going to have broad and deep disagreements with those who see themselves as sons and daughters of God.

Since the future of any civilization is leveraged on its educational structures, the battle that begins with the affirmation or denial of transcendence has been waged in education with profound intergenerational impact. In the nineteenth century, John Henry Newman already saw the import of the coming conflict about education: "Admit a God, and you introduce among the subjects of your knowledge, a fact encompassing, closing in upon, absorbing, every other fact conceivable. How can we investigate any part of any order of Knowledge, and stop short of that which enters into every order?" Newman saw that if God is ignored or rejected, "you will soon break up into fragments the whole circle of secular knowledge."[15] Our current educational regimes are now experiencing his predicted secular fragmentation of knowledge, a secularization that has produced, *pari passu*, ideological radicalization. The moral inversion that characterized Marxism, i.e., pretending to be purely scientific while masking and diverting religious moral passion, has become epidemic. The nature of the pathology makes those who suffer most from this immanentized religion at once the most radical activists for change and the most unaware of the sickness. In one way or another, human beings (nihilists excepted) will find something to be worthy of religious dedication.

Our situation is not without remedy. Christian faith remains a powerful presence. Churches across the ecclesial spectrum have continued to present the gospel that moves people from the purely immanental outlook to the clarity and happiness of the family of God. Those who attain this clarity learn to see themselves as made in the image of God, a self-understanding that instantiates the twofold worldview of transcendence interactive with immanence. The human image, very much situated in this world, is identified by its relation to the transcendent Original that is the source of this world. Believing ourselves made in God's image not only provides a basic human identity, it also grounds our moral sense, and it suggests a human role in the purposiveness of creation. If we are made in the divine image, no path apart from God could possibly lead to human fulfillment. If we are not made in the divine image, if we are not created by God, then how we live matters no more than preference or mood. The descent into darkness, begun in the late sixteenth century and culminating in the nineteenth and early twentieth centuries, at least served to illuminate the fundamental choices, all of which are still before us.

Christian faith will not remove conflict from the social, political, and economic spheres. Against the late nineteenth-century Marxist promise of a utopian world, Leo XIII warned, "It must be first of all recognized that the condition of things inherent in human affairs must be borne with, for it is impossible to reduce civil society to one dead level."[16] But Christian faith will mean that people of all classes and races—and even opponents—are to be seen as sisters and brothers. Christian faith contextualizes conflict and mollifies its urgency, because it refuses to see conflict as ultimate. However difficult the conflicts in which we may find ourselves, we have received peace "which surpasses all understanding" (Phil 4:7) from the One who has been rightly hailed as "Wonderful, Counselor, the Mighty God, the Everlasting Father, the Prince of Peace."[17] This peace can be experienced as a present state of mind, a vision of the unbroken whole, and a fervid hope for the human community.

Person and Community

The dignity that Christianity affirms in every human person stands in creative tension with the value of the community. Anarchism and nihilism dissolve the tension by losing the sense of community, leaving the individual to deal with meaninglessness in a manner of his choosing. Totalitarianism dissolves the tension by turning the individual into a mere part of the greater whole, eclipsing the value of the individual. By contrast, a sound understanding of the person avoids the two extremes, protects the value of the individual, and points toward a more balanced understanding of social groups—from the state to intervening groups like the family and various voluntary associations. And from the Christian perspective, a correct understanding of the human person is only possible if the person is conceived in relation to God. Just as Plato's carpenter could only mend the broken shuttle by envisioning its perfect form, so too are human persons and communities, whatever the particularities of their brokenness, healed by re-turning to God, in relation to whom the form and fulfillment of human wholeness is found.

Our existence is either intended by God or it is an interesting blip in an uncreated universe that neither knows nor cares that we are here. As we have repeatedly seen, when the social order is reorganized without seeing the human person as a child of God, dreadful problems have been engendered. By contrast, persisting through millennia the church has coexisted with many types of cultures and political regimes, all the while attempting to be "a sign and safeguard of the transcendence of the human person."[18] If there is any enduring import to our lives, it is because we are capable of progressively experiencing the *transcendentals*—the true, good, and beautiful. These transcendentals are the essence of the divine character, qualities of divinity that are accessible to us. They are infinite in the being of God, luminously revealed in the life and teachings of the incarnate Son, and through our relation to God, the lifeblood of the soul. Individuals and communities become more interesting, more real—more godlike—to the degree that they participate in these transcendent realities.

* * *

Since the Reformation, and especially from the Enlightenment to the present day, virtually every aspect of human life has been questioned. The age-old dispute over what it means to be human has greatly intensified. We are the descendants of Spinoza, Feuerbach, Comte, Nietzsche, and Marx; and we are also the descendants of Jewish faith and, more recently, of Jesus Christ and the church that bears his name. This discordant inheritance has brought us to an impasse about the most basic matters, since contemporary people tend to favor one or the other stream of parentage. Those who hold views diametrically opposed to faith are found among our neighbors, family members, teachers, and friends. This first volume has retraced the historical roots of late modern unbelief, its centuries-long trail of discontent, misery, and failure. And by means of this retracing, it has also pointed to the solution—the gospel that has never ceased offering its life-giving alternative.

Books 2 and 3 of *A Post-Christendom Faith* (forthcoming)

This volume, *The Long Battle for the Human Soul*, is book 1 of a set of three comprising *A Post-Christendom Faith*. Book 2, *Tradition Awakening*, will explore tradition and forces directly opposed to it, such as naturalism, Marxism, deconstruction, and unaffiliated individualism, like "spiritual but not religious." *Tradition Awakening* will begin with two conflicting visions of modernity—Nietzsche's Madman and the church's *Joy and Hope* (*Gaudium et spes*). In these competing visions, everything is at stake: our conception of the human person, the natural world, culture, and the church. Book 2 will then look at both the church and the human family as intergenerational carriers of transcendence, before proceeding to "Enclaves and Outposts: The Church in a Wilderness."

Book 3, *Theology in the Wilderness*, will set forth a Christian theology for our disoriented time. It will explore such topics as the various forms and meaning of love; the human soul; animal legacy and sin; the image of God; persons—divine and human; human distinctiveness; and the meaning of suffering, pain, and death in a good creation.

NOTES

Introduction

1 Henri de Lubac, S.J., *The Drama of Atheist Humanism*, trans. Edith M. Riley (London: Sheed and Ward, 1949), 61.

2 "Transcendence" and "immanence" have become a useful binary, a shorthand summary of religious or nonreligious outlooks. Johannes Zachhuber traces their origin to Diderot's *Encyclopédie* (1765) and their more established use to Immanuel Kant's *Critique of Pure Reason* (1781; 2nd ed., 1787). See Johannes Zachhuber, "Transcendence and Immanence," in *The Edinburgh Critical History of Nineteenth-Century Christian Theology*, ed. Daniel Whistler (Edinburgh: Edinburgh University Press, 2017), 164–81. I am indebted to Prof. Oliver Davies for calling my attention to this reference.

3 Charles Taylor, *A Secular Age* (Cambridge, Mass.: Belknap, 2007), 142–43, 374.

4 Auguste Comte, *Introduction to Positive Philosophy*, ed. and rev. trans. Frederick Ferré (Indianapolis: Hackett, 1988), 1. This book is a translation of the first two chapters of vol. 1 of Comte's *Cours de philosophie positive*.

5 C. S. Lewis, "Christian Apologetics," in *Essay Collection and Other Short Pieces*, ed. Lesley Walmsley (London: HarperCollins, 2000), 158, as cited by Walter Hooper, preface to *The Collected Letters of C. S. Lewis*, ed. Walter Hooper, vol. 2 (San Francisco: Harper San Francisco, 2004), xi.

1 Critical Turns

1 Taylor, *Secular Age*, loc. 12114, p. 539; Immanuel Kant, preface to the first edition of *Critique of Pure Reason*, trans. Norman Kemp Smith, unabridged edition (New York: St. Martin's, 1965), 9, n. a; Jacques Maritain, *Three Reformers: Luther—Descartes—Rousseau* (Westport, Conn.: Greenwood Press, 1970 [1950]), 147; and Christopher Dawson, *The Gods of Revolution*, with an introduction by Arnold Toynbee and an appreciation by James Oliver (New York: New York University Press, 1972), 63.

2 Thomas E. Woods, *How the Catholic Church Built Western Civilization* (Washington, D.C.: Regnery History, 2012), 20–21.

3 Brad S. Gregory, *The Unintended Reformation: How a Religious Revolution Secularized Society* (Cambridge, Mass.: Belknap), 2012, 139. NB: It is my practice to specify whenever I add an emphasis; otherwise, the emphasis is always in the original.

4 Gregory, *Unintended Reformation*, 140.

5 Gregory, *Unintended Reformation*, 144.

6 Gregory, *Unintended Reformation*, 141.

7 Gregory, *Unintended Reformation*, 98.

8 "Hyperpluralism" is a term first used by Gregory in *Unintended Reformation*. See Gregory, *Unintended Reformation*, 11, 74–75, 112 passim.

9 Gregory, *Unintended Reformation*, 109–10.

10 When his peace overtures failed, Luther advised, "Let everyone who can, smite, slay, and stab, secretly or openly, remembering that nothing can be more poisonous, hurtful, or devilish than a rebel. It is just as when one must kill a mad dog; if you do not strike him, he will strike you, and a whole land with you." See Sherry Jordon, "Martin Luther," in *The Christian Theological Tradition*, 4th ed., ed. Michael J. Hollerich and Mark McInroy (New York: Routledge, 2019), 355, in turn citing *Luther's Works*, 46:50; Weimar Ausgabe 18, 358.

11 Luther's two-kingdom view drew upon Jesus' statement, "Give therefore to the emperor the things that are the emperor's, and to God the things that are God's" (Matt 22:21). The affairs of the kingdom of God were not to be conflated with the right of earthly rulers to govern earthly affairs. Luther opposed the rebelling peasants because he thought they had conflated the two kingdoms. The view that there should be two independent authorities, priests and kings, had actually been anticipated long before by Pope St. Gelasius I (d. 496).

12 Gregory, *Unintended Reformation*, 160.

13 Gregory, *Unintended Reformation*, 132.

14 Gregory, *Unintended Reformation*, 160.

15 Any movement that encompasses 150 years or more of time, spreads across many nations, and engages the full gamut of human experience is likely to engender competing interpretations. Among the host of Enlightenment interpreters, two very competent but divergent

theorists are Gertrude Himmelfarb, *The Roads to Modernity: The British, French, and American Enlightenments* (New York: Vintage, 2004); and Jonathan I. Israel, *Radical Enlightenment: Philosophy and the Making of Modernity, 1650–1750* (Oxford: Oxford University Press, 2002). Himmelfarb rightly stresses that the English and American experiences of Enlightenment were markedly different from the French. Himmelfarb lists the "litany of traits" normally associated with the Enlightenment: "reason, rights, nature, liberty, equality, tolerance, science, progress," with reason heading the list. But she argues that what is conspicuously absent is *virtue*, which took precedence for the British—not personal virtue, but social virtues such as "compassion, benevolence, sympathy" (5–6). These social virtues or "social affections" were the driving force of the English Enlightenment (19). Moreover, she demonstrates the remarkable, positive impact of John Wesley's Methodist renewal and social work (116–30).

By contrast, Israel, with very good evidence, stresses the international nature of the Enlightenment. As his title indicates, Israel is particularly concerned with *radical enlightenment*. My own view is that the key national differences were primarily how religion and religious differences were handled. Radical ideas were published and discussed throughout the West; but in the midst of change, how both the dominant faith traditions and the minority faiths were treated was decisive.

16 St. Thomas Aquinas, *Summa Theologica*, trans. Fathers of the English Dominican Province (New York: Benziger Brothers, 1947), I.1.5 *sed contra*.

17 Because there was generally more intellectual freedom in the Netherlands, it makes sense that Descartes would ply his trade there. But in some tension with the Netherlands' intellectual freedom, the doctrines of its Reformed Church, especially in the prestigious Dutch universities, were considered inviolable. Trouble would ensue.

18 See Keith Hutchison, "What Happened to Occult Qualities in the Scientific Revolution?" *Isis* 73, no. 2 (1982): 233–53, https://www.jstor.org/stable/231676. Besides many other innovations, Descartes ruled out final causality: "I consider the customary search for final causes to be totally useless in physics" (*Meditations on First Philosophy*, Fourth Meditation, in *Descartes: Selected Philosophical Writings*, trans. John Cottingham, Robert Stoothoff, and Dugald Murdoch [Cambridge: Cambridge University Press, 1988], 100). Ruling out final cause or purpose in nature has been in some ways operationally useful, but the question of final cause, in such matters as the biosphere, remains controversial.

19 Descartes, *Meditations*, Fourth Meditation, 99.

20 René Descartes, *Discourse on Method*, 3rd ed., trans. Donald A. Cress (Indianapolis: Hackett, 1998 [1637]), pt. 2, p. 11.

21 Descartes' later work, *Rules for the Direction of the Mind*, #3, does allow that faith in revealed truth can take precedence over rational criteria. Additionally, his Fourth Meditation in *Meditations* offers a proof for the existence of God as what is most certain. Like many seminal figures, Descartes addresses different issues at different stages of his corpus. And like other seminal figures, Descartes is difficult to paint with a broad brush. Descartes' early work *Discourse on Method* (as have his later works) has exerted enormous influence.

22 This confidence is visible in Descartes: "Our age seemed to me to be just as flourishing and as fertile in good minds as any of the preceding ones" (*Discourse on Method*, pt. 1, p. 3).

23 Aquinas, *ST* I.1.5 *ad* 1, drawing upon Aristotle, *De Animalibus* xi.

24 The first quotation from Anselm is from chapter 1 and the second is from the preface to *Proslogium; Monologium: An Appendix in Behalf of the Fool by Gaunilo; and Cur Deus Homo*, trans. Sidney Norton Deane (Chicago: Open Court, 1903), https://sourcebooks.fordham.edu/basis/anselm-proslogium.asp. Anselm at first named this work "Faith Seeking Understanding" and did not affix his name to it. But at the urging of Hugo, Archbishop of Lyon, he did put his name to the book and also changed the title to *Proslogium*.

25 Israel, *Radical Enlightenment*, 16–18.

26 Israel, *Radical Enlightenment*, 29.

27 Israel, *Radical Enlightenment*, 39.

28 Israel, *Radical Enlightenment*, 159.

29 Baruch Spinoza, *Tractatus Theologico-Politicus*, Gebhardt Edition, 1925, 2nd ed., trans. Samuel Shirley, with an introduction from Brad S. Gregory (Leiden: Brill, 1991), 141.

30 See Israel, *Radical Enlightenment*, 232, 239.

31 Israel, *Radical Enlightenment*, 291, in turn citing G.A. Leiden, *Acta Kerkeraad* vi, res. 4 Feb. 1678; Jacob Freudenthal, *Lebensgeschichte Spinozas*, 173–74.

32 Margaret C. Jacob, *The Enlightenment: A Brief History with Documents* (Boston: Bedford/St. Martin's, 2001), 94–114. Recently discovered documents indicate that the *Treatise of the Three Imposters* was done by Jean Rousset de Missy, a leader of the Amsterdam Freemasons and one of the revolutionaries of 1747–1748; Charles Levier, a bookseller; and Jan Vroese, a lawyer who worked for the Dutch government.

33 Jacobs, *Enlightenment*, 114.

34 Jacobs, *Enlightenment*, 108.

35 Jacobs, *Enlightenment*, 109.

36 Israel, *Radical Enlightenment*, 306.

37 Immanuel Kant, *Foundations of the Metaphysics of Morals*, trans. with an introduction by Lewis White Beck (Indianapolis: Bobbs-Merrill, 1959 [1785]), 51. In a commentary that defends Kant and upholds Christian faith, John Hare explains autonomy as "appropriation, as making the moral law our own." See John Hare, *Why Bother Being Good? The Place of God in the Moral Life* (Downers Grove, Ill.: InterVarsity, 2002), 195.

38 Immanuel Kant, "What Is Enlightenment?" in *Kant on History*, ed. Lewis White Beck, trans. Lewis White Beck, Robert E. Anchor, and Emil Fackenheim (New York: Macmillan, 1989 [1784]), 8.

39 Immanuel Kant, *Religion within the Limits of Reason Alone*, trans. and with introduction and notes by Theodore M. Greene and Hoyt H. Hudson (New York: Harper and Row, 1960), 108.

40 Kant, *Reason Alone*, 188.

41 Kant, *Reason Alone*, 182–83.

42 Kant, "What Is Enlightenment?" 7.

43 Kant, "What Is Enlightenment?" 7.

44 For his argument against miracles, see David Hume, *An Enquiry Concerning Human Understanding*, esp. part X, "On Miracles," in The Harvard Classics, vol. 37 (New York: P. F. Collier and Son, 1910), 375–92.

45 Thomas Jefferson, *The Life and Morals of Jesus of Nazareth*. The work dates from around 1820 but was not published during Jefferson's lifetime. Impressively, it is written in parallel columns in Latin, Greek, French, and English.

46 *Reimarus: Fragments*, ed. Charles H. Talbert, trans. Ralph S. Fraser (Philadelphia: Fortress, 1970). See Talbert's introduction, p. 1, where he cites a contemporary account of the controversy caused by Reimarus' text.

47 *Reimarus: Fragments*, 177–97.

48 *Reimarus: Fragments*, 161.

49 *Reimarus: Fragments*, 176.

50 The impact of biblical criticism became even weightier with the work of Ernest Renan, a former seminarian who had lapsed in orthodox Catholic belief. An expert in the Semitic languages, in 1863 Renan published in French what would be a benchmark work: *The Life of Jesus*. Sympathetic to Jesus but dedicated to a rational, forensic study of Christianity, Renan considered Jesus to be "an incomparable man," but once again, not divine, not God incarnate. Within a year of its publication, Renan's *Life of Jesus* had sold fifty thousand copies, was then translated into most European languages, and became the French bestseller of the nineteenth century. Casting doubt on the historical reliability of the Bible, Renan thereby cast doubt on the veracity of the entire gospel. Like Jefferson and

Strauss, Renan considered Jesus to be a great teacher whose followers had attached legends of supernatural power to his life. That a French World War I battleship was named *Ernest Renan* indicates the extent of his influence.

51 Joseph Ratzinger, "Biblical Interpretation in Crisis: On the Question of the Foundation and Approaches of Exegesis Today: The 1988 Erasmus Lecture," *First Things*, April 26, 2008, 6, 18. I am drawing on John Martens, "Catholic Hermeneutics of the New Testament," *St. Vladimir's Orthodox Theological Quarterly* 63, no. 2 (2019): 213–35.

52 John Locke, *A Letter Concerning Toleration*, ed. James H. Tully (Indianapolis: Hackett, 1983 [1689]), 23.

53 Locke, *Letter Concerning Toleration*, 25.

54 Locke, *Letter Concerning Toleration*, 31.

55 Locke, *Letter Concerning Toleration*, 55, spelling slightly modernized.

56 Although Locke's toleration did not extend to atheists or Catholics, in more recent times, at Vatican II the Catholic Church came out clearly against all religious coercion: "This Vatican Council declares that the human person has a right to religious freedom. This freedom means that all men are to be immune from coercion on the part of individuals or of social groups and of any human power, in such wise that no one is to be forced to act in a manner contrary to his own beliefs, whether privately or publicly, whether alone or in association with others, within due limits" (*Dignitatis Humanae*, par. 2, http://www.vatican.va/archive/hist_councils/ii_vatican_council/documents/vat-ii_decl_19651207_dignitatis-humanae_en.html).

57 For an impressive list of Christian scientists and their accomplishments, see Stephen M. Barr, *Modern Physics and Ancient Faith* (Notre Dame: University of Notre Dame Press, 2003), 8–11.

58 Kant, *Critique of Pure Reason*, 9, n. a.

59 Kant, "What Is Enlightenment?" 3. Kant cites the Latin motto, *sapere aude!*, adopted by many in the German Enlightenment, which I have translated as "think boldly."

60 For a detailed account of the Revolution, see Simon Schama, *Citizens: A Chronicle of the French Revolution* (New York: Knopf, 1989).

61 The Declaration of the Rights of Man, approved by the National Assembly of France, August 26, 1789, The Avalon Project, Documents in Law, History, and Diplomacy, Yale Law School, https://avalon.law.yale.edu/18th_century/rightsof.asp.

62 Jean-Jacques Rousseau, *The Social Contract*, trans. and introduction by G. D. H. Cole (Hawthorne, Calif.: BN Publishing, 2007), 51.

63 Dawson, *Gods of Revolution*, 83, citing 84, n. 1, my emphases.

64 Michael Burleigh, *Earthly Powers: The Clash of Religion and Politics in Europe from the French Revolution to the Great War* (New York: HarperCollins, 2005), 81.
65 Dawson, *Gods of Revolution*, 75.
66 Dawson, *Gods of Revolution*, 73–74.
67 Burleigh, *Earthly Powers*, 82–83.
68 Taylor, *Secular Age*, loc. 4702, p. 204, n. 56, in turn citing from Georges Lefebvre, *Quatre-Vingt-neuf* (Paris: Editions Sociales, 1970), 245–46.
69 The new state, under the direction of the National Assembly, went further. Dawson contends that the National Assembly's attempted reformation of the French church went way beyond what Henry VIII had done in reforming the Church of England. See Dawson, *Gods of Revolution*, 67.
70 Burleigh, *Earthly Powers*, 54.
71 The plunder of church property benefited the capitalists who were able to purchase it, brokers and speculators who could resell the properties, moneylenders, rich bourgeois who bought the land, and some shopkeepers, craftsmen, and peasants with money. But the sweeping confiscation of church property did not permanently help the state, because the value of the paper money, the *assignats*, continued to fall. Many workers and others not set up to profit from plundering the church actually became impoverished, which added further fuel to the revolutionary fire, as demagogues like Marat attributed their food shortages and high prices to the aristocrats and to the royal court. The brotherhood of the original vision quickly degenerated into mob violence, social animosities, and chaos. Arnold Toynbee notes that for at least some, the Revolution was about "the sly acquisition of real estate on advantageous terms." See Dawson, *Gods of Revolution*, xi, 69.
72 Burleigh, *Earthly Powers*, 55, 85.
73 Dawson, *Gods of Revolution*, 67.
74 Burleigh, *Earthly Powers*, 65.
75 On March 10, 1791, Pius VI gave juring priests forty days to recant their oaths. See Burleigh, *Earthly Powers*, 62.
76 Burleigh, *Earthly Powers*, 96.
77 Burleigh, *Earthly Powers*, 59.
78 The royal government was not dealing with a party of political opposition, but rather with a religious movement. This religious alternative was not a mere abstraction; it was in many ways embodied in Freemasonry, which had reached its heights during the two decades before the Revolution. Freemasonry had a breadth of popularity from the ruling classes to the bourgeoisie. Many Freemasons were advocates of the Rights of Man.

They saw what they were doing as the moral and spiritual regeneration of mankind. They advocated universal peace. Anticipated in Freemasonry and in the early writings of William Blake, The Declaration of the Rights of Man became the official creed and theological foundation of the French Revolution. This religious self-understanding gave the French Revolution international appeal. See Dawson, *Gods of Revolution*, 59, 76.

79 Burleigh, *Earthly Powers*, 45.

80 Burleigh, *Earthly Powers*, 45.

81 Burleigh, *Earthly Powers*, 85.

82 Dawson, *Gods of Revolution*, 99, n. 7, citing Courtois, "Report to the Convention on the Events of 9 Thermidor." Courtois' report may be the first published use of the term "socialism."

83 Burleigh, *Earthly Powers*, 95.

84 Burleigh, *Earthly Powers*, 66.

85 Dawson, *Gods of Revolution*, 95.

86 Dawson, *Gods of Revolution*, 103.

87 Dawson, *Gods of Revolution*, 102, n. 1, my translation.

88 Dawson, *Gods of Revolution*, 63. An Italian by birth, Guiseppe Cerutti took the French nom de plume Joseph-Antoine Cerutti.

89 There are exceptions. Some Lutherans, for example, demur from any talk of progress or sanctification because of their concern that human sin would deceive and divert us. For them, even thinking about progress is dangerous and proscribed. However, the prohibition against seeking sanctification or progress has its own danger, i.e., leaving an important playing field to secular humanists.

90 Burleigh, *Earthly Powers*, 128–29.

91 Dawson, *Gods of Revolution*, 78.

92 Burleigh, *Earthly Powers*, 97.

93 Dawson, *Gods of Revolution*, 91.

94 Dawson, *Gods of Revolution*, 94.

95 For an in-depth account of the Carmelites' martyrdom, see William Bush, *To Quell the Terror: The Mystery of the Vocation of the Sixteen Carmelites of Compiègne Guillotined July 17, 1794* (Washington, D.C.: ICS, 1999), esp. 199–233.

96 Dawson, *Gods of Revolution*, 118.

97 Dawson, *Gods of Revolution*, 132.

98 Tertullian, *Apologeticus Adversus Gentes Pro Christianis*, ed. T. Herbert Bindley (Oxford: Clarendon, 1889), 152: "*semen est sanguis Christianorum.*"

99 Arnold Toynbee, introduction to Dawson, *Gods of Revolution*, x.

100 Richard Crane, professor of history, Benedictine College, in personal correspondence, September 13, 2019.

101 Dawson, *Gods of Revolution*, xv.

2 Descent into Darkness

1 Ludwig Feuerbach, *Principles of the Philosophy of the Future*, trans. Manfred H. Vogel (Indianapolis: Hackett, 1986 [1843]), 11, 29; Sergei Nechaev, "Catechism of a Revolutionist," https://pages.uoregon.edu/kimball/Nqv.catechism.thm.htm. A print version of the catechism is in Philip Pomper, *Sergei Nechaev* (New Brunswick, N.J.: Rutgers University Press, 1979), 90–94; and the Dostoevsky citation is from *Journal of an Author*, 1873, as cited in Lubac, *Drama of Atheist Humanism*, 184.

2 Samuel Taylor Coleridge, "To William Wordsworth," Poemhunter, https://www.poemhunter.com/poem/to-william-wordsworth/, spellings modernized.

3 Friedrich Schlegel, a student of Fichte, first coined the term "Romanticism." Schlegel used the term to distinguish the new expressivist style from the earlier, classical mimetic style. Because Romanticism came to include so many different authors, composers, and artists with so many different viewpoints, there is some controversy about whether the term signifies a unified movement. See Michael Allen Gillespie, *Nihilism before Nietzsche* (Chicago: University of Chicago Press, 1995), 281, n. 6. I am indebted to Gillespie's account, especially his account of Romanticism, pp. 101–34. Gillespie argues that the roots of nihilism are in the nominalism of William of Ockham (c. 1285–1347), who privileged the divine will over the divine intellect. From this medieval starting point, Gillespie traces how the tendency to prefer will over reason has affected philosophers and writers up to and including Nietzsche.

4 The Rousseau citation is from his Second Letter to Sophie, as cited in Maritain, *Three Reformers*, 148.

5 Gillespie, *Nihilism before Nietzsche*, 102.

6 Friedrich Nietzsche, *The Gay Science*, book V, §343, in *The Portable Nietzsche*, selected and trans. with an introduction, prefaces, and notes by Walter Kaufmann (New York: Penguin, 1982), 447, 448.

7 *Pastoral Constitution on the Church in the Modern World* (*Gaudium et spes*) (Boston: Pauline Books and Media, 1994 [1965]), par. 3.

8 David Friedrich Strauss, *The Life of Jesus, Critically Examined*, ed. and with an introduction by Peter C. Hodgson, trans. from the 4th German ed. by George Eliot (Philadelphia: Fortress, 1973); Ludwig Feuerbach, *The Essence of Christianity*, trans. George Eliot, introductory essay by Karl Barth, foreword by H. Richard Niebuhr (New York: Harper Torchbooks, 1957 [1841]). See also Feuerbach, *Principles of Philosophy*.

9 Feuerbach, *Principles of Philosophy*, 29.

10 Feuerbach, *Principles of Philosophy*, 68.

11 Feuerbach, *Principles of Philosophy*, 54.

12 Karl Marx, "Letter to Harman," as cited in Lubac, *Drama of Atheist Humanism*, 17.

13 Feuerbach, *Principles of Philosophy*, 71.

14 By the eighteenth century the very nature of reading had undergone an important change. A great deal of the available reading material—like novels, newspapers, and pamphlets—was designed to be consumed just once, rather than repeatedly read and reflected upon—like the Bible and devotional readings. Democratization went hand in hand with consumerism, a point first brought to my attention by Richard Crane in personal correspondence, June 9, 2020.

15 Johann Wolfgang von Goethe, *Faust, Parts One and Two*, trans. George Madison Priest (New York: Covici Friede, 1932), l. 1760, 1763. Further references to *Faust* will be done parenthetically within the text.

16 Years before *Faust* was published, Goethe had made Romantic suicide fashionable with *The Sorrows of Young Werther* (1774). See Goethe, *The Sorrows of Young Werther/Die Leiden des jungen Werther: A Dual-Language Book*, ed. and trans. Stanley Applebaum (Mineola, N.Y.: Dover, 2004).

17 *Faust* was actually written over a period of sixty years. In 1790, *Faust: A Fragment* was published and acclaimed by the Romantics. In 1808, *Faust: Part One* was published and widely read. In 1832, shortly before Goethe's death, *Faust: Part Two* was published. *Part Two* was not nearly as well received. It was seen as the work of an artist in decline. And it certainly disappointed those who would have preferred the full embrace of nihilism. See Gillespie, *Nihilism before Nietzsche*, 111.

18 Ludwig Tieck, *William Lovell* (Stuttgart: Reclam, 1986). Gillespie reads this work as a literary expression of Fichte's emphasis on the I. See Gillespie, *Nihilism before Nietzsche*, 109–10.

19 When the German composer Robert Schumann first read *Manfred*, he was tearfully overcome with emotion. Inspired by the poem, Schumann wrote incidental music for it, the most famous of which and most often played is his Overture. Schumann's response to Byron exemplifies the international, interactive nature of the Romantic movement.

20 Gillespie, *Nihilism before Nietzsche*, 123.

21 Thomas Seltzer, introduction to Ivan Turgenev, *Fathers and Sons*, trans. Constance Garnett (New York: Modern Library, n.d.), vii.

22 While *Fathers and Sons* popularized the term in 1862 Russia, the first published use of "nihilism" was probably F. L. Goetzius, *De nonismo et nihilismo in theologia* (1733). See Gillespie, *Nihilism before Nietzsche*, 65.

23 Turgenev, *Fathers and Sons*, 24.

24 Turgenev, *Fathers and Sons*, 28.

25 Turgenev, *Fathers and Sons*, 48.

26 Turgenev, *Fathers and Sons*, 34.

27 Turgenev, *Fathers and Sons*, 55–56.

28 Turgenev, *Fathers and Sons*, 56.

29 Turgenev, *Fathers and Sons*, 62.
30 Turgenev, *Fathers and Sons*, 48.
31 Turgenev, *Fathers and Sons*, 52.
32 Turgenev, *Fathers and Sons*, 77.
33 Turgenev, *Fathers and Sons*, 91.
34 Turgenev, *Fathers and Sons*, 91.
35 Turgenev, *Fathers and Sons*, 85.
36 Turgenev, *Fathers and Sons*, 96.
37 Turgenev, *Fathers and Sons*, 106.
38 Turgenev, *Fathers and Sons*, 114.
39 Turgenev, *Fathers and Sons*, 101–2.
40 Turgenev, *Fathers and Sons*, 237.
41 David Bentley Hart, "Christ and Nothing (No Other God)," in *In the Aftermath: Provocations and Laments* (Grand Rapids: Eerdmans, 2009), 17.
42 D. M. Yeager, "Confronting the Minotaur: Moral Inversion and Polanyi's Moral Philosophy," *Tradition and Discovery* 29, no. 1 (2002/2003): 22–48, esp. 25.
43 While this narrative focuses on Marxism, a similar narrative could be told about the rise of fascism. When belief in God is generally weakened and then joined with the power of the state, moral fervor does not disappear; it is displaced and concentrated into forms that cannot safely contain such moral fervor.
44 Frederick Engels, *Ludwig Feuerbach and the Outcome of Classical German Philosophy*, ed. C. P. Dutt (New York: International Publishers, 1941), 18.
45 Karl Marx, "Theses on Feuerbach," XI, in Engels, *Ludwig Feuerbach*, 84.
46 Nechaev, "Catechism."
47 Mikhail Bakunin, *God and the State*, trans. Benjamin Tucker (New York: Benjamin R. Tucker, 1895), 15, 25, as cited in Gillespie, *Nihilism before Nietzsche*, 160.
48 Burleigh, *Earthly Powers*, 303.
49 V. I. Lenin, *Essential Works of Lenin: "What Is to Be Done?" and Other Writings*, ed. and with an introduction by Henry M. Christman (New York: Dover, 1987), esp. 53–175; Nikolai Chernyshevsky, *What Is to Be Done?* trans. Michael R. Katz, annotated by William G. Wagner (Ithaca, N.Y.: Cornell University Press, 1989).
50 Gary Saul Morson, "Among the Disbelievers," *Commentary*, October 2018, https://www.commentarymagazine.com/articles/gary-morson/among-the-disbelievers/.
51 Morson, "Among the Disbelievers."
52 Michael Polanyi, *Personal Knowledge: Towards a Post-Critical Philosophy* (Chicago: University of Chicago Press, 1962), 228.
53 Polanyi, *Personal Knowledge*, 234.

54 Yeager, "Confronting the Minotaur," 23.
55 Polanyi, *The Logic of Liberty: Reflections and Rejoinders*, foreword by Stuart D. Warner (Indianapolis: Liberty Fund, 1998 [1951]), 131.
56 Polanyi, *Logic of Liberty*, 129.
57 Polanyi, *Logic of Liberty*, 129. In an excellent account, Mark T. Mitchell compares Polanyi's moral inversion to Eric Voegelin's treatment of Gnosticism. See Mitchell, *Michael Polanyi: The Art of Knowing*, in Library of Modern Thinkers (Wilmington, Del.: ISI, 2006), 144–54.
58 Polanyi, *Logic of Liberty*, 130.
59 Michael Polanyi, "Beyond Nihilism," in *Knowing and Being*, ed. Marjorie Grene (Chicago: University of Chicago Press, 1969), 4.
60 Polanyi, "Beyond Nihilism," 3.
61 Polanyi, "Beyond Nihilism," 13.
62 Yeager, "Confronting the Minotaur," 32.
63 See Polanyi, *Personal Knowledge*, 243, n. 1, drawing upon George Orwell, *Nineteen Eighty-Four: A Novel* (London: Secker & Warbur, 1949), 250.
64 Lubac, *Drama of Atheist Humanism*, ix.
65 Dostoevsky, *Journal of an Author*, 1873, cited in Lubac, *Drama of Atheist Humanism*, 184.
66 Morson, "Among the Disbelievers."
67 Morson, "Among the Disbelievers."
68 Hart, "Christ and Nothing," 18.

3 Endeavors in Darkness I

1 Lubac, *Drama of Atheist Humanism*, 77; Comte, *Positive Philosophy*, 13; Daniel J. Mahoney, *The Idol of Our Age: How the Religion of Humanity Subverts Christianity* (New York: Encounter, 2020), 4, Kindle; and Mary Pickering, "Auguste Comte," in *Love, Order, and Progress: The Science, Philosophy, and Politics of Auguste Comte*, ed. Michel Bourdeau, Mary Pickering, and Warren Schmaus (Pittsburgh: University of Pittsburgh Press, 2018), 30–60, esp. 56, https://www.jstor.org/stable/j.ctv11wk0b.
2 Comte, *Positive Philosophy*, 4.
3 Comte, *Positive Philosophy*, 13.
4 Auguste Comte, preface to *The Catechism of Positive Religion; or, Summary Exposition of the Universal Religion in Thirteen Systematic Conversations between a Woman and a Priest of Humanity*, trans. Richard Congreve (London: John Chapman, 1858), 4.

Comte signed the preface to the original French edition as "Auguste Comte, Founder of the Religion of Humanity, Sunday, 14th July, 1852" (English version, p. 38). In the original, he used his new calendar: "25th Charlemagne 64."
5 Mahoney, *Idol of Our Age*, 8.

6 Gregory, *Unintended Reformation*, 74–75, 77–78 passim.

7 Warren Schmaus, Mary Pickering, and Michel Bourdeau, "The Significance of Auguste Comte," in Bourdeau, Pickering, and Schmaus, *Love, Order, and Progress*, 30–60, esp. 11.

8 Schmaus, Pickering, and Bourdeau, "Significance of Auguste Comte," 15.

9 Schmaus, Pickering, and Bourdeau, "Significance of Auguste Comte," 12.

10 Pickering, "Auguste Comte," 47.

11 Comte, preface to *Catechism of Positive Religion*, 2.

12 Comte, preface to *Catechism of Positive Religion*, 5.

13 Comte, preface to *Catechism of Positive Religion*, 36.

14 Comte, preface to *Catechism of Positive Religion*, 5.

15 Comte, preface to *Catechism of Positive Religion*, 4, 5. Comte appropriated the aphorism from a talk by Louis Napoleon.

16 Comte, *Positive Philosophy*, 6.

17 Comte, preface to *Catechism of Positive Religion*, 1.

18 Comte, *Positive Philosophy*, 13.

19 Comte, *Positive Philosophy*, 13.

20 Comte, *Positive Philosophy*, 1.

21 Comte, *Positive Philosophy*, 2.

22 For more detailed historical accounts of final causality, see Benedict M. Ashley and James M. Jacobs, "Final Causality," in *The New Catholic Encyclopedia*, 2nd ed. (Detroit: Gale Group in association with the Catholic University of America Press, 2003). For an excellent treatment under the equivalent title "teleology," see Jeffrey Wattles, "Teleology Past and Present," *Zygon* 41, no. 2 (2006): 445–64.

23 Comte, *Positive Philosophy*, 2.

24 Comte was influenced by the earlier work of David Hume (1711–1776) and Scottish empiricism generally.

25 Comte, *Positive Philosophy*, 2.

26 Comte, *Positive Philosophy*, 8.

27 Comte, *Positive Philosophy*, 7.

28 Comte, *Positive Philosophy*, 13–14.

29 Comte, *Positive Philosophy*, 11.

30 Drawing upon Pickering, "Auguste Comte," 31.

31 Pickering, "Auguste Comte," 32.

32 Comte, *Positive Philosophy*, 6.

33 Auguste Comte, *A General View of Positivism*, trans. J. H. Bridges (Stanford, Calif.: Academic Reprints, n.d. [*Système de Politique Positive*, 1848]), 363.

34 Comte, *General View*, 438–39.

35 Comte, *General View*, 371.

36 Comte, *General View*, 378.

37 Comte, *General View*, 365.
38 Comte, *General View*, 355.
39 Comte, *General View*, 364.
40 Schmaus, Pickering, and Bourdeau, "Significance of Auguste Comte," 16.
41 Andrew Wernick, "The Religion of Humanity and Positive Morality," in Bourdeau, Pickering, and Schmaus, *Love, Order, and Progress*, 217–49, esp. 341, n. 30, citing from *Système de Politique Positive*, 1:700, trans. 565–66.
42 Cited in Lubac, *Drama of Atheist Humanism*, 102.
43 Comte, *General View*, 434.
44 Comte, *General View*, 388.
45 Lubac, *Drama of Atheist Humanism*, 102, citing E. Sémerie.
46 Lubac, *Drama of Atheist Humanism*, 85, citing Letter to M. de Tholouze.
47 Lubac, *Drama of Atheist Humanism*, 110, citing *Catéchisme* 11:353, 358; *Lettres d'Auguste Comte à divers*, 1:513; *Système de politique positive*, 3:356. English versions of Comte's new calendar can be found in *Catechism of Positive Religion*, table A and table D; see also *Auguste Comte and Positivism: The Essential Writings*, ed. Gertrude Lenzer (Chicago: University of Chicago Press, 1975), 472–73.
48 Wernick, "Religion of Humanity," 229.
49 Wernick, "Religion of Humanity," 236–37, citing Thomas Henry Huxley, *On the Physical Basis of Life* (New Haven, Conn.: The College Courant, 1869), 28.
50 Comte, *Correspondance inédite*, 2:107, as cited in Lubac, *Drama of Atheist Humanism*, 101.
51 Lubac, *Drama of Atheist Humanism*, 102. Lubac links Comte's views to Feuerbach, as well as to Alfred Loisy.
52 Comte, *General View*, 404.
53 *The Correspondence of John Stuart Mill and Auguste Comte*, ed. and trans. Oscar A. Haac, with an introduction by Angèle Kremer-Marietti (New Brunswick, N.J.: Transaction, 1995), xx, drawing on Mill, *Auguste Comte and Positivism* (1865).
54 J. S. Mill, *Autobiography*, 213, as cited in Michel Bourdeau, "Auguste Comte," in *The Stanford Encyclopedia of Philosophy*, ed. Edward N. Zalta (Summer 2018), https://plato.stanford.edu/archives/sum2018/entries/comte/. Mill coupled his critique of Comte with an insult to Ignatius Loyola, founder of the Jesuits.
55 Lubac, *Drama of Atheist Humanism*, 156.
56 The Vienna Circle, a group of various scientists and philosophers that met from about 1924 to 1936, was broadly influential in analytic philosophy. Some of their leading lights were Otto Neurath, Rudolf Carnap, and the early Ludwig Wittgenstein. A. J. Ayer, who briefly attended

their meetings, was particularly prominent in the English-speaking world. Like Comte, the Vienna Circle insisted on empirical findings as the basis of knowledge, and they completely eschewed metaphysical claims. For example, in *Language, Truth, and Logic* Ayer strongly emphasized sense experience and contended that allegedly higher claims about God or ethics lacked any valid meaning.

57 Pickering, "Auguste Comte," 56.

58 See Martin Moleski, S.J., "A Polanyian Appraisal of Outcomes Assessment: Defending the Art of Knowing against Positivist Pedagogy," *Tradition and Discovery* 45, no. 2 (2019): 5–12. In the same journal, also see Timothy L. Simpson, "Polanyian Insights on 'Professional' Teacher Preparation," 13–27.

59 Pickering, "Auguste Comte," 54.

60 Eric Voegelin, *The New Science of Politics: An Introduction* (Chicago: University of Chicago Press, 1987 [1952]), 124.

61 Voegelin, *New Science of Politics*, 7.

62 Lubac, *Drama of Atheist Humanism*, 79.

4 Endeavors in Darkness II

1 Friedrich Nietzsche, *The Antichrist*, §62, in *Portable Nietzsche*, 656; Nietzsche, "Attempt at a Self-Criticism," §5, in *Basic Writings of Nietzsche*, ed. and trans. with commentaries by Walter Kaufmann (New York: Modern Library, 1968), 23; Nietzsche, *Antichrist*, §57, p. 643; Reinhard Hütter, *Dust Bound for Heaven: Explorations in the Theology of Thomas Aquinas* (Grand Rapids: Eerdmans, 2012), 32; and Lubac, *Drama of Atheist Humanism*, 30, 62.

2 Rüdiger Safranski, *Nietzsche: A Philosophical Biography*, trans. Shelley Frisch (New York: Norton, 2002), 351–52.

3 Safranski, *Nietzsche*, 352.

4 Nietzsche, *Ecce Homo*, "Why I Am a Destiny," §1, in *Basic Writings of Nietzsche*, 782.

5 Nietzsche, *Thus Spoke Zarathustra*, Second Part, "Upon the Blessed Isles," in *Portable Nietzsche*, 198.

6 Nietzsche, *Twilight of the Idols*, "The Four Great Errors," §8, in *Portable Nietzsche*, 501.

7 Nietzsche, *Antichrist*, §47, p. 627.

8 "Zarathustra" is a more faithful rendition of the ancient Persian prophet sometimes called Zoroaster, his Hellenized name.

9 Nietzsche, *Zarathustra*, Third Part, "On Virtue That Makes Small," §3, pp. 282–83.

10 Nietzsche, *Antichrist*, §38, p. 611.

11 The book's German title can also mean "The Anti-Christian," and the book's content supports both meanings. See Walter Kaufmann, editor's

preface to *Antichrist*, 565; see also Jörg Salaquarda, "Nietzsche and the Judeo-Christian Tradition," in *The Cambridge Companion to Nietzsche*, ed. Bernd Magnus and Kathleen M. Higgins (Cambridge: Cambridge University Press, 2005), 102.

12 Nietzsche, *Antichrist*, §29, p. 601.

13 Nietzsche, *Antichrist*, §31, p. 603.

14 Nietzsche, *Zarathustra*, Second Part, "On Priests," 203.

15 Nietzsche, *Zarathustra*, Fourth Part, "The Voluntary Beggar," 384.

16 Nietzsche, *Zarathustra*, Fourth Part, "The Ass Festival," §2, p. 428.

17 Friedrich Nietzsche, *The Will to Power*, ed. with commentary by Walter Kaufmann, trans. Walter Kaufmann and R. J. Hollingdale (New York: Vintage, 1968), §1052, p. 543. This book comprises much of Nietzsche's *Nachlass*, writings and fragments unpublished before his death. His sister Elisabeth Förster-Nietzsche and his friend Peter Gast compiled and arranged the original work. His sister has been accused of questionably associating Nietzsche's work with the anti-Semites of the period.

18 Nietzsche, *Zarathustra*, Fourth Part, "The Ass Festival," §3, p. 429.

19 Nietzsche, *Zarathustra*, First Part, "Zarathustra's Prologue," §3, p. 125.

20 Nietzsche, *Antichrist*, §46, pp. 626–27.

21 Friedrich Nietzsche, "On Truth and Lie in an Extra-Moral Sense," a fragment from 1873 published posthumously, in *Portable Nietzsche*, 46–47.

22 Friedrich Nietzsche, *On the Genealogy of Morals*, trans. Walter Kaufmann and R. J. Hollingdale (New York: Vintage, 1989), Third Essay, §27, p. 161.

23 Nietzsche, *Genealogy of Morals*, Third Essay, §24, p. 152.

24 Nietzsche, *Will to Power*, §540, p. 291.

25 Nietzsche, *Antichrist*, §11, p. 577.

26 Nietzsche, *Genealogy of Morals*, First Essay, §2, p. 26.

27 Nietzsche, *Genealogy of Morals*, First Essay, §2, pp. 25–26.

28 Nietzsche, *Genealogy of Morals*, First Essay, §4–5, pp. 28–31. Nietzsche takes the German word *schlecht* (bad) to exemplify his theory, since *schlecht* "is identical with *schlicht* [plain, simple]—compare *schlechtweg* [plainly], *schlechterdings* [simply]—and originally designated the plain, the common man, as yet with no inculpatory implication and simply in contradistinction to the nobility." Nietzsche similarly presents Greek and Latin etymologies to further demonstrate and confirm the point: "good" and "bad" originate as distinctions of the powerful conquerors from the weak who have been conquered. By contrast, the powerful did not refer to powerful opponents as evil or bad.

29 Nietzsche, *Genealogy of Morals*, First Essay, §10, pp. 36–39.

30 Nietzsche, *Genealogy of Morals*, First Essay, §13, pp. 44–45.

31 Nietzsche, *Genealogy of Morals*, First Essay, §14, pp. 46–48.

32 Nietzsche, *Genealogy of Morals*, First Essay, §7, p. 33.
33 Nietzsche, *Genealogy of Morals*, First Essay, §7, pp. 33–34.
34 Nietzsche, *Genealogy of Morals*, First Essay, §8, p. 34.
35 Nietzsche, *Zarathustra*, First Part, "On the Thousand and One Goals," 171.
36 Nietzsche, *Antichrist*, I, §2, p. 570.
37 Nietzsche, *Zarathustra*, Third Part, "On Old and New Tablets," §7, p. 312.
38 Nietzsche, *Zarathustra*, Fourth Part, "The Last Supper"—"On the Higher Man," §5, p. 400.
39 Nietzsche, *Will to Power*, §968, p. 507.
40 Nietzsche, *Antichrist*, §2, p. 570.
41 Nietzsche, *Zarathustra*, First Part, Prologue, §3, p. 124.
42 Nietzsche, *Zarathustra*, First Part, Prologue, §3, pp. 124–25.
43 Nietzsche, *Zarathustra*, Third Part, §29, p. 326.
44 Nietzsche, *Zarathustra*, First Part, "On War and Warriors," 159.
45 Nietzsche, *Beyond Good and Evil*, §259, in *Basic Writings of Nietzsche*, 393.
46 Nietzsche, *Zarathustra*, First Part, "Zarathustra's Prologue," §5, pp. 129–30.
47 Nietzsche, *Zarathustra*, Third Part, "On Old and New Tablets," §21, p. 322.
48 Nietzsche, *Zarathustra*, Third Part, "On Old and New Tablets," §2, p. 305.
49 Nietzsche, *Zarathustra*, Second Part, "On the Tarantulas," 213.
50 Nietzsche, *Twilight of the Idols*, "Reason in Philosophy," §6, p. 484; *Antichrist*, §11, p. 578.
51 Nietzsche, *Will to Power*, §1067, p. 550.
52 Nietzsche, *Zarathustra*, Third Part, "The Convalescent," §2, p. 329.
53 Nietzsche, *Zarathustra*, Third Part, "The Convalescent," §2, p. 332.
54 Nietzsche, *Will to Power*, §1067, p. 550. Nietzsche sought a scientific basis to render his eternal recurrence plausible. See Safranski, *Nietzsche*, 251.
55 Nietzsche, *Will to Power*, §1066, p. 548.
56 Nietzsche, *Ecce Homo*, "Why I Am So Clever," §10, p. 258.
57 Nietzsche, *Zarathustra*, Third Part, "The Seven Seals," §1–7, pp. 340–43.
58 Nietzsche, *Zarathustra*, Third Part, "The Convalescent," §2, p. 333.
59 Nietzsche, *Zarathustra*, First Part, "On the Despisers of the Body," p. 146.
60 Tracy B. Strong, "Nietzsche's Political Misappropriation," in Magnus and Higgins, *Companion to Nietzsche*, 119–47, esp. 138.
61 Nietzsche, *Antichrist*, §42, p. 617.
62 Nietzsche, *Antichrist*, §44, p. 620.

63 Strong, "Nietzsche's Political Misappropriation," 130.
64 Safranski, *Nietzsche*, 329. That the New Testament (along with Goethe's *Faust*) was also distributed indicates an unsurprising lack of consistency, which we will not lament.
65 Burleigh, *Earthly Powers*, 444. Burleigh thinks that laying such blame on Nietzsche was a substitute for clear thinking.
66 Nietzsche, *Twilight of the Idols*, "The 'Improvers' of Mankind," §38, p. 542.
67 Nietzsche, *Ecce Homo*, "The Case of Wagner," §4, p. 779. His translator Walter Kaufmann significantly adds, "There is no period in the MS, which continued: '—or an anti-Semite.' These words were struck out, presumably not by Nietzsche" (779, n. 2).
68 Nietzsche, *Ecce Homo*, "The Case of Wagner," §3, p. 778.
69 Nietzsche, *Zarathustra*, First Part, "On the New Idol," 160–63.
70 Nietzsche, "Letter to His Sister," in *Portable Nietzsche*, 456–57.
71 Safranski, *Nietzsche*, 338.
72 Nietzsche, *Ecce Homo*, "The Case of Wagner," §4, pp. 779–80.
73 Nietzsche, *Human, All-Too-Human*, "The European Man and the Abolition of Nations," §475, in *Portable Nietzsche*, 62.
74 Nietzsche, *Will to Power*, §964, p. 506.
75 Nietzsche, *Zarathustra*, Third Part, "On Virtue That Makes Small," §3, p. 283.
76 Nietzsche, *Antichrist*, §2, p. 570.
77 Nietzsche, *Zarathustra*, First Part, Prologue, §3, p. 125.
78 David Bentley Hart, *The Beauty of the Infinite: The Aesthetics of Christian Truth* (Grand Rapids: Eerdmans, 2003), 107.
79 Hart, *Beauty of the Infinite*, 102.
80 Nietzsche, *Will to Power*, §221, p. 129.
81 Safranski, *Nietzsche*, 312, citing *B* 8:231.
82 Safranski, *Nietzsche*, 312, citing *B* 8:242.
83 Safranski, *Nietzsche*, 360.
84 Safranski, *Nietzsche*, 204, in turn citing from *B* 6:37.
85 Safranski, *Nietzsche*, 363.
86 Karl Löwith, *Nietzsche's Philosophy of the Eternal Recurrence of the Same*, trans. J. Harvey Lomax, foreword by Bernd Magnus (Berkeley: University of California Press, 1997 [1978]), 74–75, 89. Also see the excellent summary by Magnus, xv.
87 Nietzsche, *Zarathustra*, Second Part, "On the Tarantulas," 213.
88 Eric Voegelin held that Nietzsche experienced self-salvation "to the full until it broke his soul." See Voegelin, *New Science of Politics*, 174. There is a great deal of speculation, medical and otherwise, about why Nietzsche went mad and spent the last ten years of his life in something like a catatonic state.
89 Hütter, *Dust Bound for Heaven*, 32.
90 Nietzsche, *Ecce Homo*, "Why I Am a Destiny," §9, p. 335.

Conclusion

1 C. S. Lewis, *Mere Christianity* (San Francisco: Harper San Francisco, 1996), 135; Pope Leo XIII, *Rerum Novarum* (On Capital and Labor), par. 25, www.vatican.va/content/leo-xiii/en/encyclicals/documents/hf_l-xiii_enc_15051891_rerum-novarum.html.

2 Plato, *Cratylus* 389 a–b, in *The Collected Dialogues of Plato*, ed. Edith Hamilton and Huntington Cairns, trans. Benjamin Jowett, Bollingen Series LXXI (Princeton, N.J.: Princeton University Press, 1982), 421–74, esp. 427.

3 See Jerome K. Williams, *True Reformers: Saints of the Catholic Reformation* (Greenwich Village, Colo.: Augustine Institute, 2017). Williams narrates the lives and contributions of ten great Catholic Reformers in the sixteenth and early seventeenth century.

4 See Gertrude Himmelfarb, "Methodism: A Social Religion," in *Roads to Modernity*, 116–30, esp. 126.

5 Williams, *True Reformers*, 32.

6 Williams, *True Reformers*, 32, citing J. R. R. Tolkien to Christopher Tolkien, August 22, 1944, in *Letters of J. R. R. Tolkien*, ed. Humphrey Carpenter (Boston: Houghton Mifflin, 2000), 91.

7 Lewis, *Mere Christianity*, 134.

8 Immanuel Kant, *Critique of Practical Reason*, trans. with an introduction by Lewis White Beck (Indianapolis: Bobbs-Merrill, 1983 [1788]), 128.

9 Williams, *True Reformers*, 44, citing William Roper, *The Life of Sir Thomas More*, part 3 in *Two Early Tudor Lives*, ed. Richard S. Sylvester and Davis P. Harding (New Haven: Yale University Press), 1962.

10 Pope St. John Paul II similarly commented about culture: "Human beings are both child and parent of the culture in which they are immersed." See *Fides et ratio* (Boston: Pauline Books and Media, 1998), par. 71.

11 Williams, *True Reformers*, 2.

12 Aquinas, *ST* I.1.8 *ad* 2.

13 Reinhard Hütter, *John Henry Newman on Truth and Its Counterfeits: A Guide for Our Times, Sacra Doctrina Series* (Washington, D.C.: Catholic University of American Press, 2020), 68.

14 Nietzsche, *Antichrist*, §14, p. 580.

15 Hütter, *Newman on Truth*, 186, citing from John Henry Newman, *The Idea of a University Defined and Illustrated* (Oxford: Clarendon Press, 1976 [1852]), 26.

16 Pope Leo XIII, *Rerum Novarum*, par. 17.

17 Text taken from Isa 9:6, as adopted by George Frideric Handel, "For unto Us a Child Is Born," in *The Messiah*.

18 Pope St. John Paul II, *Centesimus Annus*, Encyclical Letter of Pope John Paul II on the Hundredth Anniversary of *Rerum Novarum*, 1991, par. 55, citing *Gaudium et spes*, par. 76.

BIBLIOGRAPHY

Anselm, St. *Proslogium; Monologium: An Appendix in Behalf of the Fool by Gaunilo; and Cur Deus Homo*. Translated by Sidney Norton Deane. Chicago: Open Court, 1903. https://sourcebooks.fordham.edu/basis/anselm-proslogium.asp.

Aquinas, Thomas, St. *Summa Theologica*. Translated by Fathers of the English Dominican Province. New York: Benziger Brothers, 1947.

Ashley, Benedict M., and James M. Jacobs. "Final Causality." In *The New Catholic Encyclopedia*. 2nd edition. Detroit: Gale Group in association with the Catholic University of America Press, 2003.

Barr, Stephen M. *Modern Physics and Ancient Faith*. Notre Dame: University of Notre Dame Press, 2003.

Bourdeau, Michel. "Auguste Comte." In *The Stanford Encyclopedia of Philosophy* (Summer 2018 edition), edited by Edward N. Zalta, https://plato.stanford.edu/archives/sum2018/entries/com.

Burleigh, Michael. *Earthly Powers: The Clash of Religion and Politics in Europe from the French Revolution to the Great War*. New York: HarperCollins, 2005.

Bush, William. *To Quell the Terror: The Mystery of the Vocation of the Sixteen Carmelites of Compiègne Guillotined July 17, 1794*. Washington, D.C.: ICS, 1999.

Chernyshevsky, Nikolai. *What Is to Be Done?* Translated by Michael R. Katz. Annotated by William G. Wagner. Ithaca, N.Y.: Cornell University Press, 1989.

Coleridge, Samuel Taylor. "To William Wordsworth." Poemhunter. https://www.poemhunter.com/poem/to-william-wordsworth/.

Comte, Auguste. *The Catechism of Positive Religion; or, Summary Exposition of the Universal Religion in Thirteen Systematic Conversations between a Woman and a Priest of Humanity*. Translated by Richard Congreve. London: John Chapman, 1858.

———. *A General View of Positivism*. Translated by J. H. Bridges. Stanford, Calif.: Academic Reprints [*Système de Politique Positive*, 1848].

———. *Introduction to Positive Philosophy*. Edited and revised translation by Frederick Ferré. Indianapolis: Hackett, 1988.

Dawson, Christopher. *The Gods of Revolution*. Introduction by Arnold Toynbee. An appreciation by James Oliver. New York: New York University Press, 1972.

The Declaration of the Rights of Man and of the Citizen. Approved by the National Assembly of France, August 26, 1789. The Avalon Project, Documents in Law, History, and Diplomacy, Yale Law School. https://avalon.law.yale.edu/18th_century/rightsof.asp.

de Lubac, Henri, S.J. *The Drama of Atheist Humanism*. Translated by Edith M. Riley. London: Sheed and Ward, 1949.

Descartes, René. *Discourse on Method*. 3rd edition. Translated by Donald A. Cress. Indianapolis: Hackett, 1998 [1637].

———. *Meditations on First Philosophy*, Fourth Meditation. In *Descartes: Selected Philosophical Writings*. Translated by John Cottingham, Robert Stoothoff, and Dugald Murdoch. Cambridge: Cambridge University Press, 1988.

Dostoevsky, Fyodor. *Demons*. Unabridged Garnett translation. E-Artnow, 2013 [1872].

Engels, Frederick. *Ludwig Feuerbach and the Outcome of Classical German Philosophy*. Edited by C. P. Dutt. New York: International Publishers, 1941.

Feuerbach, Ludwig. *The Essence of Christianity*. Translated by George Eliot. Introductory essay by Karl Barth. Foreword by H. Richard Niebuhr. New York: Harper Torchbooks, 1957 [1841].

———. *Principles of the Philosophy of the Future*. Translated by Manfred H. Vogel. Indianapolis: Hackett, 1986 [1843].

Gillespie, Michael Allen. *Nihilism before Nietzsche*. Chicago: University of Chicago Press, 1995.

Goethe, Johann Wolfgang von. *Faust, Parts One and Two*. Translated by George Madison Priest. New York: Covici Friede, 1932.

———. *The Sorrows of Young Werther/Die Leiden des jungen Werther: A Dual-Language Book*. Edited and translated by Stanley Applebaum. Mineola, N.Y.: Dover, 2004.

Gregory, Brad S. *The Unintended Reformation: How a Religious Revolution Secularized Society*. Cambridge, Mass.: Belknap, 2012.

Haac, Oscar A., ed. and trans. *The Correspondence of John Stuart Mill and Auguste Comte*. Introduction by Angèle Kremer-Marietti. New Brunswick, N.J.: Transaction, 1995.

Hare, John. *Why Bother Being Good? The Place of God in the Moral Life*. Downers Grove, Ill.: InterVarsity, 2002.

Hart, David Bentley. *The Beauty of the Infinite: The Aesthetics of Christian Truth*. Grand Rapids: Eerdmans, 2003.

———. "Christ and Nothing (No Other God)." In *In the Aftermath: Provocations and Laments*, 1–19. Grand Rapids: Eerdmans, 2009.

Himmelfarb, Gertrude. *The Roads to Modernity: The British, French, and American Enlightenments*. New York: Vintage, 2004.

Hollerich, Michael J., and Mark J. McInroy, eds. *The Christian Theological Tradition*. 4th edition. New York: Routledge, 2019.

Hütter, Reinhard. *Dust Bound for Heaven: Explorations in the Theology of Thomas Aquinas*. Grand Rapids: Eerdmans, 2012.

———. *John Henry Newman on Truth and Its Counterfeits: A Guide for Our Times. Sacra Doctrina Series*. Washington, D.C.: Catholic University of America Press, 2020.

Hume, David. "On Miracles." In *An Enquiry Concerning Human Understanding*, 289–420. The Harvard Classics, vol. 37. New York: P. F. Collier and Son, 1910.

Hutchison, Keith. "What Happened to Occult Qualities in the Scientific Revolution?" *Isis* 73, no. 2 (1982): 233–53. https://www.jstor.org/stable/231676.

Israel, Jonathan I. *Radical Enlightenment: Philosophy and the Making of Modernity, 1650–1750*. Oxford: Oxford University Press, 2002.

Jacobs, Margaret C. *The Enlightenment: A Brief History with Documents*. Boston: Bedford/St. Martin's, 2001.

John Paul II, Pope St. *Centesimus Annus*. Encyclical Letter of Pope John Paul II on the Hundredth Anniversary of *Rerum Novarum*, 1991.

———. *Fides et ratio*. Boston: Pauline Books and Media, 1998.

Kant, Immanuel. *Critique of Practical Reason*. Translated with an introduction by Lewis White Beck. Indianapolis: Bobbs-Merrill, 1983 [1788].

———. *Critique of Pure Reason*. Unabridged edition. Translated by Norman Kemp Smith. New York: St. Martin's, 1965.

———. *Foundations of the Metaphysics of Morals*. Translated with an introduction by Lewis White Beck. Indianapolis: Bobbs-Merrill, 1959 [1785].

———. *Religion within the Limits of Reason Alone*. Translated with an introduction and notes by Theodore M. Greene and Hoyt H. Hudson. New York: Harper and Row, 1960.

———. "What Is Enlightenment?" In *Kant on History*, edited by Lewis White Beck, translated by Beck, Robert E. Anchor, and Emil Fackenheim, 3–10. New York: Macmillan, 1989 [1784].

Lenin, V. I. *Essential Works of Lenin: "What Is to Be Done?" and Other Writings*. Edited and with an introduction by Henry M. Christman. New York: Dover, 1987.

Lenzer, Gertrude, ed. *Auguste Comte and Positivism: The Essential Writings*. Chicago: University of Chicago Press, 1975.

Leo XIII, Pope. *Rerum Novarum* (On Capital and Labor). www.vatican.va/content/leo-xiii/en/encyclicals/documents/hf_l-xiii_enc_15051891_rerum-novarum.html.

Lewis, C. S. *The Collected Letters of C. S. Lewis*. Vol. 2. Edited by Walter Hooper. Harper San Francisco, 2004.

———. *Mere Christianity*. San Francisco: Harper San Francisco, 1996.

Locke, John. *A Letter Concerning Toleration*. Edited by James H. Tully. Indianapolis: Hackett, 1983 [1689].

Löwith, Karl. *Nietzsche's Philosophy of the Eternal Recurrence of the Same*. Translated by J. Harvey Lomax. Foreword by Bernd Magnus. Berkeley: University of California Press, 1997 [1978].

Mahoney, Daniel J. *The Idol of Our Age: How the Religion of Humanity Subverts Christianity*. New York: Encounter, 2020. Kindle.

Maritain, Jacques. *Three Reformers: Luther—Descartes—Rousseau*. Westport, Conn.: Greenwood Press, 1970 [1950].

Martens, John. "Catholic Hermeneutics of the New Testament." *St. Vladimir's Orthodox Theological Quarterly* 63, no. 2 (2019): 213–35.

Marx, Karl. "Theses on Feuerbach." In Frederick Engels, *Ludwig Feuerbach and the Outcome of Classical German Philosophy*, 82–84. Edited by C. P. Dutt. New York: International Publishers, 1941.

McLellan, David. *Karl Marx: His Life and Thought*. Frogmore, St. Albans, England: Paladin, 1977.

Mitchell, Mark T. *Michael Polanyi: The Art of Knowing*. In Library of Modern Thinkers. Wilmington, Del.: ISI, 2006.

Moleski, Martin, S.J. "A Polanyian Appraisal of Outcomes Assessment: Defending the Art of Knowing against Positivist Pedagogy." *Tradition and Discovery* 45, no. 2 (2019): 5–12.

Morson, Gary Saul. "Among the Disbelievers." *Commentary*, October 2018. https://www.commentarymagazine.com/articles/among-the-disbelievers/.

Nechaev, Sergei. "Catechism of a Revolutionist." https://pages.uoregon.edu/kimball/Nqv.catechism.thm.htm.

Newman, John Henry. *The Idea of a University Defined and Illustrated*. Oxford: Clarendon Press, 1976 [1852].

Nietzsche, Friedrich. *The Antichrist*. In *The Portable Nietzsche*, selected and translated with an introduction, prefaces, and notes by Walter Kaufmann, 565–656. New York: Penguin, 1982.

———. "Attempt at a Self-Criticism." In *Basic Writings of Nietzsche*, translated and edited with commentaries by Walter Kaufmann, 17–27. New York: Modern Library, 1968.

———. *Beyond Good and Evil*. In *Basic Writings of Nietzsche*, translated and edited with commentaries by Walter Kaufmann, 179–435. New York: Modern Library, 1968.

———. *The Gay Science*. In *The Portable Nietzsche*, selected and translated with an introduction, prefaces, and notes by Walter Kaufmann, 93–102. New York: Penguin, 1982.

———. *Human, All-Too-Human*. In *The Portable Nietzsche*, selected and translated with an introduction, prefaces, and notes by Walter Kaufmann, 51–64. New York: Penguin, 1982.

———. "Letter to His Sister." In *The Portable Nietzsche*, selected and translated with an introduction, prefaces, and notes by Walter Kaufmann, 456–57. New York: Penguin, 1982.

———. *On the Genealogy of Morals*. Translated by Walter Kaufmann and R. J. Hollingdale. New York: Vintage, 1989.

———. "On Truth and Lie in an Extra-Moral Sense." In *The Portable Nietzsche*, selected and translated with an introduction, prefaces, and notes by Walter Kaufmann, 42–47. New York: Penguin, 1982.

———. *Thus Spoke Zarathustra*. In *The Portable Nietzsche*, selected and translated with an introduction, prefaces, and notes by Walter Kaufmann, 103–439. New York: Penguin, 1982.

———. *Twilight of the Idols*. In *The Portable Nietzsche*, selected and translated with an introduction, prefaces, and notes by Walter Kaufmann, 463–563. New York: Penguin, 1982.

———. "Why I Am a Destiny." In *Ecce Homo*, in *Basic Writings of Nietzsche*, translated and edited with commentaries by Walter Kaufmann, 782–91. New York: Modern Library, 1968.

———. *The Will to Power*. Translated by Walter Kaufmann and R. J. Hollingdale, edited with commentary by Walter Kaufmann. New York: Vintage, 1968.

Orwell, George. *Nineteen Eighty-Four: A Novel*. London: Secker & Warbur, 1949.

Pickering, Mary. "Auguste Comte." In *Love, Order, and Progress: The Science, Philosophy, and Politics of Auguste Comte*, edited by Michel Bourdeau, Mary Pickering, and Warren Schmaus, 30–60. Pittsburgh: University of Pittsburgh Press, 2018. https://www.jstor.org/stable/j.ctv11wk0b.

Plato. *Cratylus*. In *The Collected Dialogues of Plato*, edited by Edith Hamilton and Huntington Cairns, translated by Benjamin Jowett. Bollingen Series LXXI. Princeton, N.J.: Princeton University Press, 1982.

Polanyi, Michael. "Beyond Nihilism." In *Knowing and Being*, edited by Marjorie Grene, 3–23. Chicago: University of Chicago Press, 1969.

———. *The Logic of Liberty: Reflections and Rejoinders*. Foreword by Stuart D. Warner. Indianapolis: Liberty Fund, 1998 [1951].

———. *Personal Knowledge: Towards a Post-Critical Philosophy*. Chicago: University of Chicago Press, 1962.

Pomper, Philip. *Sergei Nechaev*. New Brunswick, N.J.: Rutgers University Press, 1979.

Ratzinger, Joseph. "Biblical Interpretation in Crisis: On the Question of the Foundation and Approaches of Exegesis Today: The 1988 Erasmus Lecture." *First Things*, April 26, 2008.

Reimarus: Fragments. Edited by Charles H. Talbert. Translated by Ralph S. Fraser. Philadelphia: Fortress, 1970.

Roper, William. *The Life of Sir Thomas More*. Part 3 in *Two Early Tudor Lives*, edited by Richard S. Sylvester and Davis P. Harding. New Haven: Yale University Press, 1962.

Rousseau, Jean-Jacques. *The Social Contract*. Translated with an introduction by G. D. H. Cole. Hawthorne, Calif.: BN Publishing, 2007.

Safranski, Rüdiger. *Nietzsche: A Philosophical Biography*. Translated by Shelley Frisch. New York: Norton, 2002.

Salaquarda, Jörg. "Nietzsche and the Judeo-Christian Tradition." In *The Cambridge Companion to Nietzsche*, edited by Bernd Magnus and Kathleen M. Higgins, 90–118. Cambridge: Cambridge University Press, 2005.

Schama, Simon. *Citizens: A Chronicle of the French Revolution*. New York: Knopf, 1989.

Schmaus, Warren, Mary Pickering, and Michel Bourdeau. "The Significance of Auguste Comte." In *Love, Order, and Progress: The Science, Philosophy, and Politics of Auguste Comte*, edited by Michel Bourdeau, Mary Pickering, and Warren Schmaus, 3–24. Pittsburgh: University of Pittsburgh Press, 2018. https://www.jstor.org/stable/j.ctv11wk0b.

Simpson, Timothy L. "Polanyian Insights on 'Professional' Teacher Preparation." *Tradition and Discovery* 45, no. 2 (2019): 13–27.

Spinoza, Baruch. *Tractatus Theologico-Politicus*. Gebhardt Edition, 1925. 2nd edition. Translated by Samuel Shirley with an introduction by Brad S. Gregory. Leiden: Brill, 1991.

Strauss, David Friedrich. *The Life of Jesus, Critically Examined*. Edited and with an introduction by Peter C. Hodgson. Translated from the 4th German edition by George Eliot. Philadelphia: Fortress, 1973.

Strong, Tracy B. "Nietzsche's Political Misappropriation." In *The Cambridge Companion to Nietzsche*, edited by Bernd Magnus and Kathleen M. Higgins, 119–47. Cambridge: Cambridge University Press, 2005.

Taylor, Charles. *A Secular Age*. Cambridge, Mass.: Belknap, 2007.

Tertullian. *Apologeticus Adversus Gentes Pro Christianis*. Edited by T. Herbert Bindley. Oxford: Clarendon, 1889.

Tieck, Ludwig. *William Lovell*. Stuttgart: Reclam, 1986.

Tolkien, J. R. R. *Letters of J. R. R. Tolkien*. Edited by Humphrey Carpenter. Boston: Houghton Mifflin, 2000.

Turgenev, Ivan. *Fathers and Sons*. Translated by Constance Garnett. Introduction by Thomas Seltzer. New York: Modern Library, n.d.

Vatican II. *Dignitatis Humanae*. http://www.vatican.va/archive/hist_councils/ii_vatican_council/documents/vat-ii_decl_19651207_dignitatis-humanae_en.html.

———. *Pastoral Constitution on the Church in the Modern World* (*Gaudium et spes*). Boston: Pauline Books and Media, 1994 [1965].

Voegelin, Eric. *The New Science of Politics: An Introduction*. Chicago: University of Chicago Press, 1987 [1952].

Wattles, Jeffrey. "Teleology Past and Present." *Zygon* 41, no. 2 (2006): 445–64.

Wernick, Andrew. "The Religion of Humanity and Positive Morality." In *Love, Order, and Progress: The Science, Philosophy, and Politics of Auguste Comte*, edited by Michel Bourdeau, Mary Pickering, and Warren Schmaus, 217–49. Pittsburgh: University of Pittsburgh Press, 2018. https://www.jstor.org/stable/j.ctv11wk0b.

Williams, Jerome K. *True Reformers: Saints of the Catholic Reformation*. Greenwich Village, Colo.: Augustine Institute, 2017.

Woods, Thomas E. *How the Catholic Church Built Western Civilization*. Washington, D.C.: Regnery History, 2012.

Yeager, D. M. "Confronting the Minotaur: Moral Inversion and Polanyi's Moral Philosophy." *Tradition and Discovery* 29, no. 1 (2002/2003): 22–48.

Zachhuber, Johannes. "Transcendence and Immanence." In *The Edinburgh Critical History of Nineteenth-Century Christian Theology*, edited by Daniel Whistler, 164–81. Edinburgh: Edinburgh University Press, 2017.

INDEX OF NAMES AND SUBJECTS

INDEX OF SCRIPTURE